THE LAST ADAM

THE LAST ADAM
A Study in Pauline Anthropology

ROBIN SCROGGS

Fortress Press   Philadelphia

Library of Congress Catalog Card No. 66-23416

FOREWORD

Many teachers and colleagues have contributed to such merit as this book may possess by their encouragement, suggestions, and criticisms. Chief among these has been Professor W. D. Davies of Union Theological Seminary in New York. Mr. Davies first suggested to me that I undertake the study and his constant support and friendship over the intervening years deserve more acknowledgement of gratitude than is possible here. I owe thanks also to Professors R. B. Y. Scott and Franklin Young, both of Princeton University, to Professor Wayne Rollins of Wellesley College, and to my colleague at Dartmouth, Professor Jacob Neusner. To Ruth, my wife, goes particular thanks for her careful typing of the manuscript and the encouragement she unceasingly gives. Whatever faults lie in these pages belong to me alone.

Grateful acknowledgement is made to the following publishers for permission to quote copyrighted material in the present volume: to Oliver and Boyd, Edinburgh, for passages from *Christ and Adam*, by Karl Barth; to Clarendon Press, Oxford, for passages from *The Apocrypha and Pseudepigrapha of the Old Testament*, edited by R. H. Charles; and to Harvard University Press, Cambridge, for passages from the Loeb Classical Library translation of the works of Philo, edited and translated by F. H. Colson, G. H. Whitaker, and R. Marcus.

Easter, 1966   ROBIN SCROGGS
Hanover, N.H.

ABBREVIATIONS

AJSL	*The American Journal of Semitic Languages and Literature*
ARN	*Aboth de Rabbi Nathan*
BASOR	*Bulletin of the American Schools of Oriental Research*
C.N.T.	'Commentaire du Nouveau Testament'
ET	*Expository Times*
H.N.T.	'Handbuch zum Neuen Testament'
H.N.T.C.	'Harper's New Testament Commentary'
IB	*The Interpreter's Bible*
I.C.C.	'International Critical Commentary'
j	*Talmud Jerushalmi*
JBL	*Journal of Biblical Literature*
JTS	*Journal of Theological Studies*
Koh.Z.	*Koheleth Zuta*
K.E.K.	'Kritisch-exegetischer Kommentar', founded by H. A. W. Meyer
LXX	Septuagint
M.	*Mishnah*
Mek	*Mekilta*, ed. Lauterbach
Mid. Teh.	*Midrash Tehillim*, ed. Buber
M.N.T.C.	'Moffatt New Testament Commentaries'
MRK	*Myth, Ritual, and Kingship*, ed. S. H. Hooke
N.T.D.	'Das Neue Testament Deutsch'
NTS	*New Testament Studies*
Pesik.	*Pesikta de Rab Kahana*, ed. Mandelbaum
Pesik. R.	*Pesikta Rabbati*, ed. Friedmann
P.R.E.	*Pirke de Rabbi Eliezer*
R.	After abbreviation of Old Testament book, designates *Midrash Rabbah*
RB	*Revue Biblique*
RGG	*Die Religion in Geschichte und Gegenwart*. 3d edition
RHPR	*Revue d'Histoire et de Philosophie Réligieuses*
RSV	*Revised Standard Version* of the Bible and Apocrypha
S.B.T.	'Studies in Biblical Theology'
SJT	*Scottish Journal of Theology*
T	*Tosephta*

Tanh.	Midrash Tanhuma
Tanh. B.	Midrash Tanhuma, ed. Buber
Targ. Jon.	Targum Jonathan
Targ. Jer.	Targum Jerushalmi
Targ. Onk.	Targum Onkelos
ThL	Theologische Literaturzeitung
ThZ	Theologische Zeitschrift
TWNT	Theologisches Wörterbuch zum Neuen Testament, ed. Gerhard Kittel
WZKM	Wiener Zeitschrift für die Kunde des Morgenlandes
ZAW	Zeitschrift für die Alttestamentliche Wissenschaft
ZNW	Zeitschrift für die Neutestamentliche Wissenschaft
ZTK	Zeitschrift für Theologie und Kirche

Abbreviations of tractates of the Talmud are those used in the index volume (pp. 1–2) of the Soncino translation of *Talmud Babli* edited by I. Epstein, *The Babylonian Talmud* (London, 1935–52). Definitions and explanations of some of the rabbinic terms used in the text will be found in the glossary of the Soncino index volume. Unless otherwise indicated, translations of rabbinic materials are my own.

Qumran manuscripts are designated according to the standard system adopted in D. Barthelemy, J. T. Milik, et al., *Qumran Cave I: Discoveries in the Judaean Desert I* (Oxford, 1955).

5

23

29

TABLE OF CONTENTS

INTRODUCTION

This study is directed toward a specific motif of Paul's Christology: Christ, the Last Adam. Paul believes that the eschatological age has been inaugurated by a man who embodies God's intent for all men—an intent thwarted by the first Adam, fulfilled by the Last. No one ought to underestimate the originality of the Apostle as he attempts to make clear the unique significance of the one man Jesus Christ. At the same time no one can deny that Paul speaks out of an understanding informed by language and concepts of the religious traditions of his day. Paul is, at least, a Jew in the Graeco-Roman world. Thus to understand Paul's 'Adamic Christology' (the name given to the motif in this study), we must evaluate motifs in other traditions which seem to have been known to him. Yet the eclecticism of Paul, or at least of his age, makes the correct selection of the most important background a precarious task. The notorious number of attempts to explain Paul from this or that religion is well-known and needs no elaboration here.

Nevertheless, hardly any doubt can exist that Paul well knew Jewish theology about Adam. Most scholars would, I believe, agree that this thought has decisively influenced his Adamic Christology. Yet the problem of understanding Paul's background is not so easily solved, for the question arises whether Jewish theology has taken over motifs and meanings of outside traditions. In recent years the most prevalent answer has been in the affirmative. Judaism has absorbed into its Adamic thought speculation, usually called 'gnostic', about a glorious first creature, the *Urmensch*. Many religions are said to have exemplified, or at least contributed to, the conception of such a mythical creature. Evidence is drawn from Indian, Persian, Jewish, Christian, and Islamic sources, as well as from religions and writings more explicitly gnostic (e.g., the Hermetica). That the final description of this myth is composite and exists as a whole in no single tradition does not deter scholars from using this description to explain details in whatever ancient tradition they are studying, even though the tradition itself could not be called gnostic (e.g., Judaism or Christianity).[1] What this

[1] A description of the composite myth may conveniently be found in Rudolf Bultmann, *Primitive Christianity in its Contemporary Setting* (New York, 1957), pp. 163f.

Urmensch is said to be and do may vary, but he is at least a glorious figure and usually bears some relationship to, if not identity with, the figure of a savior. Hence in some circles the *Urmensch* has been popularly called the 'Saved-Savior'.

The validity of the methodology involved and its results can be questioned; most recently Carsten Colpe has explicitly attacked what he considers the too facile conclusions of such an approach.[2] Colpe sums up the claims of this pan-religious theory. It asks us to believe that 'the gnostic savior myth arose sometime in the misty past, somewhere in the vast reaches of the Orient, which can only a little more precisely be identified as "Iran". It wandered then through space and time, left behind mosaics at one time or another in this or that circle of tradition, e.g., in Wisdom poetry, Philo, Adamic speculation, and apocalyptic, then grew together again in Manichaeism to a grandiose unity, and finally with the Mandaeans disintegrated into its separate parts.'[3] The purpose of the present study is not, however, to attack the theory of the *Urmensch*-savior.

What is important here is that this composite picture of the *Urmensch* has been used to interpret Jewish thought about Adam. The basic study was made by Benjamin Murmelstein in two articles in the late 1920's.[4] The conclusions reached by Murmelstein have been accepted by many scholars, often it would seem to me, without any critical test of his methodology.[5] An independent, but somewhat similar, study was made by Willi Staerk in 1938.[6]

Murmelstein stakes out a broad area in religious thought, encompassing Christian, Jewish, Jewish-gnostic, and Islamic texts, covering many centuries. When all these are put together, he believes it possible to discern a view of Adam and the Savior

---

[2] Carsten Colpe, *Die religionsgeschichtliche Schule* (Göttingen, 1961).
[3] Ibid., p. 191.
[4] 'Adam, ein Beitrag zur Messiaslehre,' *WZKM*, XXXV (1928), 242–75, continued in XXXVI (1929), 51–86. Cf. Colpe, *Schule*, pp. 56f.
[5] Note the frequency of footnote references to Murmelstein's articles in later studies, studies which assume the accuracy of Murmelstein's conclusions; e.g., *TWNT*, I, 141; Bultmann, 'Ursprung und Sinn der Typologie als hermeneutischer Methode,' in *Pro Regna Pro Sanctuario*, eds. W. J. Kooiman and J. M. Van Veen (Nijkerk, 1950), p. 92, n. 17; Oscar Cullmann, *The Christology of the New Testament* (Philadelphia, 1959), p. 144, n. 3.
[6] *Die Erlösererwartung in den Östlichen Religionen: Soter II* (Stuttgart, 1938), pp. 7–138.

that became prominent in Christianity but which was mediated to Christianity by Judaism. According to Murmelstein this view is influenced in one way or another by the old myth of the *Urmensch*, which he believes stems ultimately from India.[7] As it appears in Judaism and Christianity, the *Urmensch* and the Savior each represents a different age: the one, a golden age of the past; the other, the hoped for age of the future. Since, however, the future age is seen in terms of the original, the two figures come to have similar forms and functions.[8] Indeed, the Savior becomes Adam himself. This *Urmensch*-Savior contains all souls within himself[9] and is king, high priest, and prophet.[10] While Murmelstein occasionally uses the term 'ideal' of these figures,[11] it is not entirely clear just what he considers the function of this myth to be: that is, whether the figures simply represent for Judaism a kind of humanity, or whether they are considered particular, 'historical' men who bring into existence (i.e., 'save') the humanity they also represent. The latter, however, seems to be the case. This would mean that all the attributes ascribed to Adam or Messiah pertain to the concrete figures themselves, so that the theologians are drawing verbal images of how they believe these 'men' actually were or will be. Once the soteriological function of the truly existent *Urmensch* is established, all the Jewish descriptions of the glorious Adam seem to fall into place. Adam is glorified because he is the Savior.

To follow Murmelstein's argument throughout his entire exposition is impossible here. Yet the issues of methodology and interpretation are so crucial that some inspection is necessary. Consequently I want to describe briefly just one section: his discussion of texts which, he believes, relate Adam to the Messiah. Adam has sinned and brought death to all men.[12] One of Adam's descendants will make good the sin and nullify its results.[13] A logion in *Gen. R.* XXIV.4 interprets Isa. 57:16 in the following manner: '*For I will not contend forever*—with Adam—*nor will I always be angry*—with his descendants—*for a Spirit* [ruah]

---

[7] *WZKM*, XXXV (1928), 247.   [8] Ibid., 246f.
[9] Ibid., 261–68.   [10] Ibid., 268–75.
[11] E.g., *WZKM*, XXXVI, (1929), 86.
[12] Cf. Bar. 48:42; *B.B.*17a; *Koh. Z.*, par. 43; Murmelstein, *WZKM*, XXXV (1928), 253.
[13] *WZKM*, XXXV (1928), 254.

will go out from me.'[14] Murmelstein identifies this Spirit as the
Messiah on the basis of another logion found, among other
places, in *Yebamoth* 62a.[15] Thus the Messiah is the descendant
of Adam who will nullify the anger of God against mankind. In
support of this conclusion Murmelstein cites a logion (*Exod. R.*
XXX.3) which states that in the days of the Messiah God will
bring an end to death, a penalty upon man originating with Adam.
The famous passage in T. Levi 18 demonstrates a continuation of
this thought.

> In his [the priest-messiah's] priesthood shall sin come to an
> end
> And the lawless shall cease to do evil.
> And he shall open the gates of paradise,
> And shall remove the threatening sword against Adam.
> And he shall give to the saints to eat from the tree of life,
> And the spirit of holiness shall be on them.
> And Beliar shall be bound by him.[16]

Now the Messiah places Adam back into paradise. 'The salvation
of Adam is complete.'[17]

According to Murmelstein, the identification of the *Urmensch*
with the Savior is most clearly to be seen in *Num. R.*
XIII.12 (and parallels). Due to Adam's sin six things have been
lost, to be regained only when the Messiah comes. These six
things are the light of Adam's countenance (i.e., his glory), his
size, his life, the fruit of the earth, paradise, and the sun and moon.
For the understanding of the *Urmensch*-Savior, the most important
of these returning goods are those of the countenance and size of
Adam. The Messiah reveals this wonder in his own person. 'He
is a second Adam.'[18]

Only the final step is missing: the assertion that Adam is
himself the coming savior. This step is not to be found in extant
rabbinic sources, although hints that the idea once existed can in
fact be discovered. Since early Christian theology had raised the

---

[14] So Murmelstein's translation; the Hebrew of the last clause reads,
‏כִּי רוּחַ מִלְפָנַי יַעֲטוֹף‎.

[15] *WZKM*, XXXV (1928), 254.

[16] T. Levi 18:10–12. Unless otherwise noted, translations of the Pseudepigrapha are taken from *Apocrypha and Pseudepigrapha of the Old Testament*,
ed. R. H. Charles (Oxford, 1913).

[17] *WZKM*, XXXV (1928), 255.   [18] Ibid., 258.

identity of the two Adams to a place of great importance, it was necessary that this identification be suppressed in Judaism.[19] The traces that Murmelstein finds of this rejected teaching are the following. *Gen. R.* XXI.7 interprets Ps. 17:5 as being the voice of David: 'When he who was created according to your image awakes, I shall behold your face in righteousness.' This seems to indicate that Adam is the eschatological judge, and this role can only be adequately explained if Adam is also the Savior.[20] A second trace is to be found in a logion which pictures Adam giving 70 of his determined 1,000 years of life to David, since he learns that David had been given only three hours to live.[21] But the word 'David' really indicates the Messiah (so *Megillah* 17*b*). Thus 'David is the Messiah; he has, however, no life of his own; he has the life of Adam.'[22]

Hardly any step in the above argument can go unchallenged.[23] Murmelstein's attempt to read *ruaḥ* in *Gen. R.* XXIV.4 as 'Spirit' and to make this refer to the Messiah cannot be sustained. In the first place, *ruaḥ* in the midrash is taken to mean 'wind', not 'spirit'. The rabbis who constructed the midrash, as well as the biblical author, did not understand the passage to have anything to do with the Messiah. In the second place, the assertion that *Yebamoth* 62*a* refers to the Messiah by the word *ruaḥ* (spirit) is also not justified. *Yebamoth* 62*a* reads as follows:

> For R. Assi stated: The Son of David will not come before all the souls in *Guρ* [literally, 'body'] will have been disposed of, since it is said, *For the spirit [ruaḥ] that unwrappeth itself is from Me* [Isa. 57:16].[24]

Ruaḥ refers here to the individual soul which resides in the *guρ* until it begins its historical existence. As will be seen in chapter III, *guρ* can hardly refer to Adam. The saying in *Exodus Rabbah* XXX.3 does contrast the results of Adam's sin with the recovery of the originally intended good in the messianic age. Adam and Messiah, however, are not themselves brought into any direct parallelism or contrast. It is, in fact, God who restores

[19] Ibid., 258f.   [20] Ibid., 259.   [21] *Num. R.* XIV.
[22] *WZKM*, XXXV (1928), 260.
[23] Detailed exegesis of many of these texts will be found in Chapters II and III below. At the moment only the inconsistencies in Murmelstein's argument can be noted.
[24] Translation that of *The Babylonian Talmud*, ed. I. Epstein, (London: Soncino Press, 1935).

man's good, *in the days of* the Messiah. T. Levi 18 does make the Messiah an active agent in the restoration,[25] but even here Adam is no personal figure in the eschatological drama. The saints are those who are to eat from the tree of life, and the use of the name Adam is really a reference to mankind, not to the 'historical' Adam who appears again. Certainly nothing is said about leading Adam back into paradise nor about completing the salvation of the first man.

The logion Murmelstein believes expresses most clearly the *Urmensch*-Savior myth (*Num. R.* XIII.12) shows rather that the author finds it impossible to marshal conclusive evidence. What is lost is mankind's good. Nothing is said about Adam's recovering this good. While it may be implied that the Messiah would himself be arrayed in Adam's original nature, surely the point of the whole saying is directed not to any specific mythic figure, be he Adam or Messiah, but toward man himself. If this is the clearest passage Murmelstein can adduce for a 'Second Adam', then what has really been proved is that rabbinic theology knows of no such figure.

The argument that the key identification between Adam and Messiah is lacking only because of its emphasis in Christianity thus becomes a desperate attempt. Purely aside from the questionable statement that Christianity made such an identification, not to speak of its becoming a cardinal motif, Murmelstein's practice of explaining away gaps and silences by attributing them to reaction against Christianity is hardly justifiable without evidence of such reaction, particularly when his pages are mostly devoted to showing how many parallels and similarities there are! But what about traces of the identification which the author believes he has found in Judaism? The logion in *Gen. R.* XXI.7 may show a belief in a personal life for Adam at the eschatological day, but even if it does, Adam is here primarily a symbol for mankind in its freedom from the decree of death. How Murmelstein can believe the passage implies a role for Adam as judge is completely mystifying. The second argument is equally untenable. Adam's gift of 70 years of his life to David arises not out of a conception of the *Urmensch* but out of exegetical wrestling with a scriptural

---

[25] This text is almost without parallel in Jewish literature of the period. It may, in fact, be a Christian interpolation; cf. Chap. II. below.

anomaly. God threatens to punish Adam with death on the day
he eats of the forbidden fruit; yet Scripture records that he lived
930 years (Gen. 5:5). The difficulty is partially solved by the
psalmist's equation of a day of the Lord with 1,000 years of human
time. But now Adam has a surplus of 70 years. Seeing that David
is assigned only three hours of life, Adam gallantly gives up 70
years so that the king can live a full life span. No doubt 'David'
at times refers to Messiah, but that the name does so in this logion
is impossible. Is the Messiah to live only 70 years? To say that
the Messiah lives the life of Adam is completely irrelevant to the
intent of the logion.

The conclusion can only be drawn that Murmelstein's argument is unacceptable. He has produced no evidence that leads
one to the judgment that Jewish theologians took over a teaching
of an *Urmensch*-Savior. That he is forced to ignore contexts, to
put materials together that have no intrinsic relationship, and to go
far beyond the reasonable meaning of the texts he uses suggests
that the approach he has followed and the conclusions reached are
not drawn out of the texts themselves but are placed upon them.
If Paul's Adamic Christology is inspired by teaching of an
Urmensch-Savior, the inspiration does not derive from apocalyptic
or rabbinic Judaism.[26]

A variation of Murmelstein's attempt to encompass the Adamic
myths within the broad pattern of an *Urmensch*-Savior is the
suggestion that the Adamic myth is a sub-category of the myth of
the Son of Man. More specifically it is claimed that Paul's
Christology of the Last Adam is really a Son of Man Christology.
This claim so determines criteria of interpretation that again a
brief look at the argument is necessary. Oscar Cullmann may be
taken as an example of a recent exponent.[27]

Cullmann asks why the redeemer figure in some Jewish
speculation is called 'Man'.[28] His answer is that the concept of the
Son of Man had its origin in non-Jewish speculation about an

---

[26] Or, for that matter, from Hellenistic Judaism; cf. Addendum II below.
Recent attempts to relate the gnostic Savior myth to Judaism have tended to
concentrate on the wisdom speculation of the post-Old Testament period (cf.
the clear statement by Wilckens in *TWNT*, VII, 508–14). Since in his Adamic
Christology Paul uses no wisdom motifs, this issue cannot be discussed here.

[27] *The Christology of the New Testament*, Chap. VI, esp. pp. 137–53, 166–81.

[28] Ibid., pp. 142, 144. Cullmann accepts the judgment that Aramaic
barnasha simply means 'man'.

Original Man. In those circles the identification of the ideal heavenly man with the first man led to the belief that the first man would actually redeem mankind.[29] In Judaism this identification was avoided because it conflicted with the indigenous notion that the first man brought sin, not salvation, into the world.[30] As a result, the original speculation split into two separate lines, one concerning the Original Man and one concerning the redeemer figure, now called the Son of Man, 'So that their original solidarity is no longer apparent.'[31] Cullmann nevertheless finds Jewish tradition wrestling with the problem of the original unity of the motifs and describes these attempts as the 'Adam problem'.[32] For Judaism there were two possible solutions: either to put no emphasis upon the identification of the figures, or to put no emphasis upon Adam's sin.[33] With regard to the latter possibility, Cullmann notes that I Enoch stresses the figure of the Son of Man while ignoring the sin of Adam. Here he asks, 'Has not the author at least unconsciously still remembered that . . . the barnasha who returns at the end is identical with the first man?'[34]

Cullmann believes that Paul's Christology is to be understood in the light of the above development. The Apostle too has a solution to the 'Adam problem'. He uses only the motifs of the Jewish first man (as distinct from the motif of the Son of Man), yet he is really interested in the incarnate heavenly man who will return in the end time (that is, in Jesus as the Son of Man).[35] Thus Paul proposes a unique solution which overcomes the problems left unsolved by earlier Jewish attempts.

Much of Cullmann's argument clearly implies acceptance of the *Urmensch*-Savior myth and its influence upon Jewish thought. But apart from this, is it necessarily the case that the original situation and use of a term gives the basic clue to its present meaning regardless of intervening time and development? Indeed, Cullmann seems to suggest that the original identity of first man and heavenly man exists inherently even in the separated motifs. No matter how rigidly Jewish theology isolated these factors, later theologians were forced to wrestle with a possible reunion, albeit perhaps 'unconsciously'.[36] I believe that the origin of the

---

[29] Ibid., p. 143.   [30] Ibid., p. 144.   [31] Ibid.
[32] Ibid.   [33] Ibid., p. 145.   [34] Ibid., p. 146.
[35] Ibid., p. 166.   [36] Ibid., p. 146.

Son of Man speculation in Judaism is still in doubt. But granted for a moment that both Son of Man and Adam stem from the myth of a Primeval Man, the crucial question is how the motifs are used in their new environment. As early as Daniel these two myths would have been separated. After two hundred years of this separation there is no necessity to assume that Paul *had* to wrestle with the 'Adam problem'. Nor does the name, Son of *Man*, force the conclusion that Jewish theologians were always aware that a Primeval Man was an essential ingredient in the concept. There is indeed a problem connected with the Adamic motifs in Judaism, and Cullmann rightly notes how the view of Adam as first sinner is often altered. But is this to be attributed to the 'Adam problem?' In the chapters below I will try to suggest that the change is due to an 'anthropological problem'. Some Jewish theologians avoided the concept of a sinful Adam, not because it conflicted with a foreign notion of an ideal Primeval Man, but because by means of the exalted Adam they could more easily describe God's intent for man and for Israel.

If one still wishes to find an *Urmensch*-Savior directly behind Paul's thought about the Last Adam, he must appeal either to gnosticism proper or to a gnostically-influenced early Christianity. The former possibility has at times been suggested, but not many scholars have been willing to accept it in an unqualified form.[37] Purely apart from the vexing problem of the date of gnosticism proper,[38] this view cannot convincingly show historical or substantival lines of relationship between such gnosticism and the

[37] Some commentators are quite ready to accept a strong gnostic background for the Apostle but are reticent about suggesting how Paul came into contact with this background, e.g., E. Käsemann, *Leib und Leib Christi* (Tübingen, 1933), pp. 163–68, and R. Bultmann, *New Testament Theology*, I (New York, 1954), pp. 174, 251. R. Reitzenstein, in his first edition of *Die hellenistischen Mysterienreligionen*, claims that Paul must have read directly Hellenistic religious literature (cited by W. G. Kümmel, *Das Neue Testament: Geschichte der Erforschung seiner Probleme* [Freiburg, 1958], p. 341); but by the second edition (Leipzig, 1920; p. 257) he has accepted Bousset's argument of a prior Hellenistic Christianity which mediated to Paul the Hellenistic-gnostic ideas.

[38] Scepticism about a genuine pre-Christian gnosticism will always remain until earlier sources are uncovered. That such a gnosticism could have existed, however, is eminently possible and perhaps probable; cf. the recent studies by E. Haenchen, 'Gab es eine vorchristliche Gnosis?', *ZTK*, XLIX (1952), 316–49; U. Wilckens, *Weisheit und Torheit* (Tübingen, 1959), pp. 97–213, and his article in *TWNT*, VII, 508–14; D. Georgi, 'Der vorpaulinische Hymnus Phil. 2, 6–11,' in *Zeit und Geschichte*, ed. E. Dinkler (Tübingen, 1964), pp. 263–93. At the present stage of understanding, the final criterion must be found in the similarities of functions and motifs, not in the uncertainties of dating.

B

Apostle. Paul by his own admission was first so fanatically Jewish
and then so fanatically Christian, while always so opposed to
paganism, that it is impossible to imagine his coming into serious
intellectual discussion with either a gnostic community or writing.
The increasing awareness of the pervasive influence of Judaism
and early Christianity on Paul both in totality[39] and detail[40]
inclines one rather in the opposite direction.

Much more difficult to judge, but inherently more likely, is
the possibility that Paul made contact with an early gnostic
Christianity. For our purposes this problem becomes crucial
because of the disturbances at Corinth, which many exegetes
believe were caused by gnostically-influenced Christians.[41] With
regard to Paul's Adamic Christology the question can be narrowed
further to a discussion of I Cor. 15, where Paul is said to
be arguing against a gnostic view of immortality.[42] The assumption of gnosticism in Corinth is open to some question, but the
issues cannot be discussed here.[43] One could, at any rate, accept
the gnostic background of the Corinthians without believing in
turn that Paul's Adamic Christology was gnostically influenced.

Just such an assumption of a gnostic influence on Paul is,
however, the real beginning point for the careful and somewhat
complicated study of Rom. 5:12–21 by Egon Brandenburger.[44]
Paul, he contends, has utilized the Corinthian Christology of the
Urmensch-Savior, although he has corrected it in I Cor.
15 and later in Rom. 5. To be sure, the corrections Paul makes
radically alter the originally gnostic meaning, and Rom. 5:12–21

[39]Although W. D. Davies' work *Paul and Rabbinic Judaism* (2d ed.; London,
1954) has not found such wide acceptance in German scholarship as it has in
England and Scandinavia, many German exegetes are nevertheless moving
toward a greater acceptance of the importance of Judaism in Paul's Christian
thinking, particularly with regard to apocalyptic. Cf. the recent studies of
E. Käsemann, 'Gottesgerechtigkeit bei Paulus,' *ZTK*, LVIII (1961), 367–78;
'Zur Thema der urchristlichen Apokalyptik,' *ZTK*, LIX (1962), 278–84;
C. Müller, *Gottes Gerechtigkeit und Gottes Volk* (Göttingen, 1964); and U.
Wilckens, 'Die Bekehrung des Paulus als religionsgeschichtliches Problem,'
ZTK, LVI (1959), 273–93.

[40]E. g., the increasing awareness of the midrashic quality of his argumen-
tation as well as the omnipresence of Christian liturgical phrases.

[41]E.g., in recent years, Bultmann, *TWNT*, I, 709–11; W. Schmithals,
Die Gnosis in Korinth (Göttingen, 1956); Wilckens, *Weisheit*.

[42]E.g., Schmithals, pp. 71–74; E. Schweizer, *TWNT*, VI, 417f.

[43]Cf. my article, 'The Exaltation of the Spirit by Some Early Christians,'
JBL, LXXXIV (1965), 370–73.

[44]*Adam und Christus: Exegetisch-religionsgeschichtliche Untersuchung zu
Römer 5, 12–21* (Neukirchen, 1962).

becomes through these corrections a complex of gnostic, apoca-lyptic, and Jewish-juridical language, all initiated into the service of the Christian proclamation.[45] Thus in an important way Brandenburger guards against the dangers to which some too-facile gnostic interpretations fall prey. Nevertheless, because Brandenburger begins with gnostic theology, he misses the main thrust of the Pauline argument.

According to Brandenburger, Paul in I Cor. 15 fights against a group which believes it has already won immortality. The Apostle, on the contrary, emphasizes the resurrection as purely future.[46] His opponents have contrasted the pneumatic Christ, and therefore the pneumatic Christian, to the natural (ψυχικός) Adam, who represents unsaved humanity.[47] Branden-burger finds the origin of this thought world in various gnostic materials, for example Zozimus, Poimandres, the Naassene and Mandean writings.[48] Paul himself shares enough of the pre-suppositions of this mythology so that he can use the Corinthian Adamic Christology as the basis of discussion, although his correction really shatters the center of the gnostic view.[49] Why, however, Paul should use a conception he must immediately alter in its essentials remains unclear throughout Brandenburger's book.[50]

In Rom. 5:12 Paul returns to the Corinthian Christology. Brandenburger believes that Paul repeats gnostic ideas in 12a-c, for these phrases imply that all mankind is under a fate or power which first fell upon the *Urmensch*.[51] Once Paul reaches 12c he becomes aware of a possible misunderstanding. With the addition of 12d, 'Because all have sinned', Paul avoids the danger of determinism by asserting the Jewish notion of individual responsi-bility.[52] Following an article by Bornkamm, Brandenburger sees the anacoluthon at the end of verse 12 as a significant theological moment and further evidence of Paul's awareness of the need for

---

[45] Ibid., p. 247.   [46] Ibid., pp. 70f.
[47] Ibid., pp. 73f.   [48] Ibid., pp. 77–109.
[49] Ibid., p. 75.
[50] So also a question raised by E. Jüngel, 'Das Gesetz zwischen Adam und Christus,' *ZTK*, LX (1963), p. 58. Jüngel's general critique of Brandenburger is very instructive.
[51] Brandenburger strongly denies 12a–c could represent a genuinely Jewish view; *Adam und Christus*, p. 161.
[52] Ibid., pp. 176ff.

correction.[53] Instead of completing the Adam/Christ correspondence Paul breaks off his sentence and introduces instead two parentheses. The first (vss. 13f.) deals with the question of responsible sin in relation to the Torah. The second (vss. 15–17) safeguards the implied correspondence from any further misunderstanding by showing the incomparability of the figures.[54] Only now in verses 18f. can Paul safely make the correspondence he began in verse 12. Brandenburger insists 18f. must be read in the light of the corrections Paul has interspaced since verse 12.[55]

With this correspondence Paul initiates a new interpretation of the work of Christ. The motifs of covenant and people of God are now broadened into the category of universal history. The work of Christ is now no more simply a passing by of former sins (Rom. 3:25) but a freeing from the powers of sin and death themselves. That is, the work of Christ has effected a change of Lordship.[56] Paul guards against the inherent gnostic substantival change of Lordship (the obtaining of a new *nature* from the Savior) by historicizing the event of the fall and by interpreting the saving act of Christ in terms of the doctrine of justification.[57]

An adequate critique of Brandenburger's very detailed study cannot be given in a few paragraphs; the real basis of disagreement can only unfold in the constructive sections of the following chapters. Yet the most crucial problems can at least be mentioned here.

1. The argument that the motif of correspondence between Adam and Christ is taken by Paul from the Corinthians is more asserted than proved by Brandenburger. There is, in fact, no real evidence for the assertion. Against it is that the entire complex woven around the motif in I Corinthians 15 is composed of elements crucial to Paul. (a) The resurrection. Whether the Corinthian theology was gnostic or not, the resurrection of the body was not part of its teaching. Needless to say, it is an essential Pauline emphasis. (b) Ἐν τῷ Χριστῷ. This motif appears in I Corinthians 15:22 and almost certainly determines the ἐν τῷ Ἀδάμ of the same verse. Again a key motif of Paul. (c) Christ as source

<hr/>

[53] Ibid., p. 158; cf. G. Bornkamm, 'Paulinische Anakoluthe im Römerbrief,' in *Das Ende des Gesetzes* (2d ed.; Munich, 1958), pp. 80–90.

[54] Brandenburger, *Adam und Christus*, pp. 219–31.

[55] Ibid., p. 243. [56] Ibid., pp. 237f. [57] Ibid., pp. 238f.

of the resurrection life. Discussion of this will follow in chapter V, but here attention can be called to texts such as Phil. 3:21, Col. 3:4, and II Cor. 3:18. (d) The life-giving Spirit. The Spirit is elsewhere for Paul the means of the resurrection life; compare II Cor. 3:18 and Rom. 8:11. (e) Christ as image (εἰκών). Compare II Cor. 4:4 and Col. 1:15. (f) The new existence as a bearing or wearing of the new garment. Brandenburger argues that I Cor. 15:49 is related to the motif of the putting on of the garments of immortality.[58] 'Just as we have borne the image of the earthly man, let us also bear the image of the heavenly.' If this is correct, another frequently recurring Pauline image is present.[59] The whole context of the Adamic Christology in I Cor. 15 is indissolubly tied to these essential Pauline motifs.

2. Brandenburger finds in I Cor. 15:21f. and Rom. 5:12 ideas which he mistakenly claims are foreign to 'genuine Judaism'. I Cor. 15:21f. asserts that death came to the world because of Adam. Jewish examples of this belief are numerous and well-known.[60] Rom. 5:12 is more complicated because both death and sin are issues. Sin entered the world through Adam and because of this sin he died. This is all that 12a–b asserts, and it is a commonplace of Jewish theology. Adam's history is in 12c–d related to that of all men (here is the real correspondence in verse 12): because all men sin, they too die. As will be seen, this is also a prominent, albeit not universal, judgment of Jewish thought. Not only is this verse entirely consonant with Jewish theology, but also any link with specific gnostic motifs (that is, motifs which separate gnosticism from other kinds of thinking) is extremely difficult to see. Perhaps a gnostic Christian could affirm what Paul says in I Cor. 15:21f., but since a Jewish Christian could do the same, these verses cannot be used in and of themselves to argue for a gnostic background for the motif of the correspondence. It is even doubtful whether such a gnosticism could have made the link between sin and death that Paul makes in Rom. 5:12a–b, not to speak of 12c–d. In summary: One must argue against Brandenburger that Paul's Adamic Christology is based securely in Jewish theology about Adam and in Paul's own

[58] Ibid., pp. 139f.
[59] As Brandenburger also acknowledges, ibid., p. 140, n. 1.
[60] Cf. below, pp. 18 and 36.

theological concerns. This means in turn that Rom. 5:12*d* and following are not corrections but a continuation of a unified sequence that has its roots not simply in 12*a-c* but in 5:1–11 as well.

3. Although terms of rulership are indeed present in Rom. 5:12–21, it is hardly justified to argue that the change of lordship is the key motif. Death and sin rule on the one hand (vss. 14, 17, 21). But what one would expect Paul to contrast with the rulership of death and sin, should change of lordship be the theme, is entirely missing. Christ as Lord appears only in the stereotyped liturgical end of the entire section.[61] Nowhere is Christ said to be the ruler of the new kingdom. Rather grace or the believers themselves rule (vss. 17, 21). The motif of Christ's enthronement so central to the passage in Phil. 2:5–11, where change of lordship is the theme, is also missing.

The fact is, Brandenburger has failed to see that the central concern of the entire Pauline Adamic Christology is eschatological anthropology. Very consistently he relegates to a brief excursus the Jewish anthropological materials which provide the real clue to the Adamic Christology.[62] By reading gnostic Savior mythology into I Cor. 15, he obviates the fact that here the new humanity as such is Paul's primary interest. Although Rom. 5 cannot be simply equated with I Cor. 15, its ultimate purpose is also to speak of the eschatological life of the believer, and this means his new humanity as given him by the one true man, Jesus Christ.[63] Nor does Brandenburger's steady movement away from the gnostic motif of an *Urmensch*-Savior draw him any closer to a correct interpretation of Paul. Indeed in one respect he is further away at the end than at the beginning, for Paul shares with the gnostics at least a strong interest in eschatological anthropology. Brandenburger rightly senses a difference between Paul and gnosticism, but this difference lies not in Paul's absence of anthropological interest in his Adamic

---

[61] Cf. similar conclusions in 5:11, 6:23, 7:25, and 8:39.

[62] Brandenburger, *Adam und Christus*, pp. 135–39.

[63] Entirely consonant with Brandenburger's dependence upon gnostic categories is his failure to see the insights in Barth's exegesis of Romans 5, *Christ and Adam* (Edinburgh, 1956); cf. Brandenburger, *Adam und Christus*, pp. 267–78. Certainly not all of Barth's exegesis is justifiable, and his curious use of non-eschatological language to speak of what are, for Paul, eschatological verities is potentially misleading. Nevertheless, Barth's anthropological understanding of the Adamic Christology *is* basically justified.

Christology, but rather in the description of what the new humanity is and how it is realized.[64]

So many questions are raised by these attempts to understand Paul and the Judaism contemporary to him that one readily sees the need for an interpretation which has its center in the texts themselves. The primary task in studying Jewish theology and Paul is to determine first their own framework and their own intent, to grasp the meaning they ascribe to a motif by seeing how it functions in their own theological context. I have attempted to follow this priority in the present work. The meaning of a saying or a complex of sayings is to be determined by its use in context. Obviously no one can be satisfied that a simple recital of the mythic story is an adequate explanation of its meaning. It is, however, just as inadequate to trace the material to some presumed source and to claim without careful inspection that the meaning of the present tradition is the same as that of its original context. Little attention is given in this study to possible sources of the traditions. What has been considered crucial is the function the material serves within its present context.

No doubt at some specific points questions arise as to possible origin in Hellenistic or gnostic traditions. Unless, however, the function as well as the form of the tradition has been transferred to the new situation, discussion of origin is largely irrelevant in determining the meaning of the saying as presently used. Once the basic meaning is found, points of possible contact with other traditions can then be studied. But to begin with outside traditions is to begin at the wrong end.

What this study attempts to do is to view early Jewish theology of Adam from the perspective outlined above. Primary attention is focused on the use which the material serves within the theological framework of Judaism. Paul is then studied from this theological framework to see the use he makes of the Adamic myth. Just at this point, however, the eclecticism of the Apostle raises a question about such a methodology. Is it justifiable to consider Paul's Jewish background as truly 'inside'? That is, is the attempt

---

[64] There are, of course, other viewpoints on the relation of Paul to gnosis and related influences, but space limitations prohibit a discussion here or in the following chapters. In the final analysis the best argument for a constructive alternative is not a negative attack on other positions but a coherent and persuasive positive statement. This much the coming chapters hope to provide.

to understand Paul from the standpoint of his Jewish heritage imposing an outside set of criteria which might prejudice the true meaning of his Christology? No one can deny that much, at least, of the Adamic material is taken by Paul from Judaism. Nevertheless, that Judaism is 'inside' Paul's theological perspective is, it must be admitted, an assumption of this study. What I hope to show is that this judgment leads to a coherent structuring of the Apostle's thought. Whether the interpretation given in these pages is more or less coherent than other possibilities must in the final analysis be left to others to decide. At no point do I want to insist that Paul is guided and influenced only by his Jewish and Christian heritage. I do believe that the basic coherence found in Paul by this study suggests that in the main his Adamic Christology is primarily directed by his awareness and reinterpretation of Jewish Adamic myths. Both in Judaism and in Paul hints of Hellenistic and gnostic traditions are likely to be found. Such hints, however, in no way endanger the basic understanding, unless they are found to be so numerous and to exist at such crucial points that the Jewish framework itself is called in question. My study has led me to the conclusion that this question does not need to be called.

CHAPTER I

OLD TESTAMENT THOUGHT OF THE FIRST ADAM

Genesis 2:4b–4:1

Although there is much uncertainty at present about source criticism of the Tetrateuch, Gen. 2:4*b*–4:1 certainly is very ancient. While the final form of the myth about Adam probably dates from the time of the united kingdom, the stories themselves go back well into the second millenium B.C. That the myth of Adam in its present form contains dissimilar and contradictory elements is notorious, and attempts to isolate and explain these elements form a long and famous chapter in the history of source-criticism. Two basic positions have emerged. Instigated by the scholarship of Karl Budde, the most venerable view is that behind the present form of the myth lie two parallel accounts of the same story, skillfully woven together by the final compiler.[1] Each separate account contains both a creation and a paradise story. Other scholars, however, argue that two different myths, one about creation and the other about paradise, form the bases for the Yahwist's final narrative. Here particularly is to be noted the careful monograph of Paul Humbert.[2] For reasons which cannot be effectively argued here, I am convinced that the latter view is correct, and I acknowledge a heavy debt to the searching analysis of Humbert.[3] The creation story attempts to explain the origin of man and asserts the first man's exalted stature and positive

[1] Karl Budde, *Die biblische Urgeschichte* (Giessen, 1883), and more recently, *Die biblische Paradiesesgeschichte* (Giessen, 1932); also J. Begrich, *ZAW*, IX (1932), 93ff.; H. Gunkel, *Genesis* (3d ed.; Göttingen, 1910), pp. 5ff.; Hans Schmidt, *Die Erzählung von Paradies und Sündenfall* (Tübingen, 1931), pp. 4ff. (Schmidt also believes a creation myth underlies part of the final myth).

[2] Paul Humbert, *Études sur le récit du paradis et de la chute dans la Genèse* (Neuchatel, 1940), pp. 48–81; also A. Lods, *RHPR*, XXV (1945), 71–78; H. Gressmann, 'Die Paradiessage,' in *Festgabe A. von Harnack* (Tübingen, 1921), pp. 24–42.

[3] For a complete investigation of this problem, cf. my doctoral thesis, 'The Adamic Christology of Paul in the Light of His Jewish Heritage' (Princeton University, 1962), Appendix A. My analysis differs in some details from that of Humbert.

relation to God. This source is found in 2:4*b*–7, 9*a*, 15, 18–24; 3:20f., 23; and 4:1.[4] The myth of the lost paradise narrates that primeval act which resulted in man's present precarious and critical condition. This source is contained in 2:8, 9*b*, 16f., 25; 3:1–19, 22 and 24.[5] We shall examine each of these in turn.

THE MYTH OF CREATION

At the time of Yahweh Elohim's making of earth and heaven— before any shrub of the field was on the earth and before any herb had sprouted, for Yahweh Elohim had not sent rain upon the earth nor was there any man to till the arable soil—a flood used to go up out of the earth and would water all the face of the soil. Then Yahweh Elohim molded the man (out of dust)[6] from the arable soil, and he breathed into his nostrils breath of life; thus the

---

[4] Gen. 2:18–24 is a recognizable unit in which the prominent themes are those of creation and the '*adamah*, the 'arable soil'. To this unit can then be joined related verses. Gen. 2:4*b*–7 contains both creation and '*adamah* themes. Verse 9*a* again concerns creation out of the '*adamah* and is to be separated from 9*b* for reasons both of syntax and content. Verse 15 must be added here because it is a clear doublet to verse 8, a verse which belongs to the paradise story. Humbert thinks that here the word *gan*, 'garden', has displaced an original '*adamah;* cf. *Études*, p. 54. While this suggestion satisfies grammatical difficulties in the text, it probably is not necessary. The garden motif became attached to the periphery of the creation story prior to the final joining of the myths. Verse 3:20 belongs here because it continues the positive view of sex contained in the creation account. Double names for people and gods are not unusual in Near Eastern mythology. The double naming of Eve is thus more likely to derive from the expansion of oral tradition than from the existence of two separate sources. Verse 3:21 belongs here because it is a continuation of the beneficence of Yahweh so clearly seen in the creation account and because it appears to be a real doublet of 3:7, a verse which belongs in the paradise myth. Verse 3:23 belongs because it fulfills the lack described in 2:5. Verse 4:1 also probably belongs; it contains the only other appearance of *ḥawwah* outside of 3:20 and demonstrates again the creation story's positive emphasis upon sex and procreation. Verse 4:1 can be argued as originally independent of the Cain and Abel story which follows; cf. Mowinckel, *The Two Sources of the Predeuteronomic Primeval History (JE) in Gen.* 1–2 (Oslo, 1937), pp. 37–42.

[5] The central unit here is 3:1–19. With the exception of the series of curses it forms a carefully constructed and unified section. Verses 2:16f. and 3:22 and 24 obviously belong with this unit. Verse 2:8 is the nearest thing we have to a beginning of the garden story. Verse 9*b*, because of its motif, is to be added to verse 8. Verse 2:25 can be seen as a link created by the redactor to join more smoothly the creation with the paradise story (cf. J. McKenzie, *Theological Studies*, XV [1954], 560), but there is no real reason to exclude it from the paradise account. What may be redactional is the frequent use of the relative clause to tie together the various elements of the two myths, e.g., 8*b*, 'whom he had formed,' and 3:1, 'that the Lord God had made.' This construction is prominent throughout both chapters, and Begrich labels it a stylistic characteristic of the Yahwist; cf. *ZAW*, IX, (1932), 102.

[6] Perhaps to be excised as a gloss.

man became a living creature. Yahweh Elohim made to sprout from the soil every tree which was pleasant in appearance and good for food, and Yahweh Elohim took the man and placed him in the garden of Eden to till and guard it.

But Yahweh Elohim said: 'It is not good for the man to be by himself; I shall make for him an aid which corresponds to him.' Then Yahweh Elohim molded from the soil every beast of the field and every bird of the heaven and he brought them to the man to see what he would call them. And every name which the man called each living creature became its name. Thus the man named the names of each animal, and bird of heaven, and beast of the field; but for the man he did not find an aid which corresponded to him.

Then Yahweh Elohim caused a trance to fall upon the man; and he slept. He took one of his ribs and then closed flesh beneath it. And Yahweh Elohim fashioned the rib he had taken from the man into a woman, and he brought her to the man. The man said: 'This is it! Bone of my bones and flesh of my flesh. Woman shall she be called, for from a man was she taken.' (This is the reason a man will forsake his father and his mother and shall cleave to his woman and they shall become one flesh.) The man called the name of his woman 'Eve'—for she was to become[7] the mother of all living.

Then Yahweh Elohim made for the man and his woman tunics of skin, and he dressed them. Yahweh Elohim sent him out from the garden of Eden to till the soil from which he had been taken. The man had intercourse with Eve, his woman. She conceived and gave birth to Cain, and she said: 'I have acquired a man with the help of Yahweh.'

The creation myth in Gen. 2ff. shares a theology of creation-salvation with an important Near Eastern tradition, according to which salvation, i.e., the present blessings of life and fertility, has been bestowed through the order which the gods have created out of disorder, or chaos.[8] Von Rad suggests that the Yahwist uses

---

[7] The use of the perfect to express a future situation regarded from the standpoint of the speaker as an accomplished fact.

[8] Cf. Henri Frankfort, et al., *The Intellectual Adventure of Ancient Man* (Chicago, 1946), published in Great Britain as *Before Philosophy* (Harmondsworth, Middlesex, 1951), and Ivan Engnell, *Studies in Divine Kingship in the Ancient Near East (Uppsala, 1943).*

the myth to push the beginning of *Heilsgeschichte* back to creation, and this can only mean that creation is itself an act of salvation.[9] There is harmony between Yahweh's intention and the result of his acts. The conclusion of the myth finds man naturally fulfilling the ends his God has set for him in creation. No hint can be found of the dark side of sex and work, a motif so prominent in the myth of paradise. Man turns obediently to work on the soil, while woman joyfully brings forth a son and gives credit to God for the gift of this new life.

Our main concern, however, is the form and function of 'the man'[10] in this myth. The following are his essential characteristics.

1. *Nature*. The man is created from two already existing 'substances', moistened soil and the breath of Yahweh. In distinction from the animals only man has in him the *nešamah*, the breath of Yahweh. This not only makes man unique in the created order; it also gives him an intimate relationship to the creator god.[11] The notion may be seen as the counterpart of Gen. 1:26f., where God creates man in the image and likeness of the divine beings.

2. *Wisdom*. This important characteristic of the man is implied in his naming the animals and woman rather than explicitly stated. In ancient thought the name is considered to be of the essence of the thing named, so that the act of naming indicates a wisdom great enough to perceive the essence of the object.[12] Thus the first man in the Genesis myth could not name the animals unless he knew the essence or 'soul' of the creatures.[13]

3. *Work*. The man is destined to be a tiller of the soil. Gen. 2:5 implies this, while 2:15 and 3:23 indicate that he apparently proceeded to this destiny naturally and without question.

4. *Sexual awareness*. A striking feature of the creation myth is that it is preoccupied with the centrality of sex and procreation in human life. The animals are created in the hope that an aid

[9] Von Rad, *Old Testament Theology*, I (New York, 1962), 138f.
[10] Mention hardly needs to be made of the fact that in Gen. 2f. *'adam* is not a proper name. The first man is, in name, still a prototype.
[11] So Gunkel, *Genesis*, p. 6. But cf. Gen. 7:22, where the *nešamah* seems to belong to every living creature, whether man or animal.
[12] Cf. *TWNT*, V, 242f., and, as examples, *Enūma eliš*, VI, lines 5–8; Ps. 147:4f.; Isa. 40:26.
[13] Cf. J. Pedersen, *Israel I–II* (London, 1926), pp. 245, 259, and Humbert, *Études*, p. 57.

might be found for the man, and the narrative suggests that the function of the aid is that of sexual partner. Verses 2:23f. deal with the aetiology of sex; 3:20 explains the name of the woman in terms of her function of begetting; 4:1 describes the first birth cycle, thus demonstrating that one of the man's functions is to be the father of the human race. He accepts sex, even rejoices in it, as one of the created goods of life.

5. *Mortality*. The myth does not appear to be concerned with the problem of immortality, as does the myth of paradise. The creation narrative describes the origin of the present order, without suggesting any dichotomy between what once was and what now exists. In all likelihood the myth understands that the first man was subject to death.

The individual traits of the first man in the creation myth can clearly be seen. To describe his basic form and function is not as easy, but I believe it probable that he is portrayed implicitly as a king.[14] The most decisive argument for this view lies in the fact that the man participates in the main event with which the myth is concerned. That is, the function of the man is determined by the function of the myth: the description of the bestowal and continuation of the salvation of creation. He has a royal function and therefore a royal form. It is crucial to note that it is by means of the man that Yahweh completes his creative work, the fertility of the fields and the procreation of humankind. The only serious problems here are the absence of explicit references to the man's royalty and the flavor of a primitive situation of the man.[15] The figure of the man has become more or less altered during the centuries of tradition-transmission which the myth has undergone. The royal function, nevertheless, has remained to indicate the original form of the first man.

[14] The argument depends upon the description of the original man in terms of the politico-religious mythology of the reigning king, the so-called 'king ideology'. For a classic description cf. Engnell, *Divine Kingship*. The king is the possessor of great wisdom. In this wisdom he rules and dispenses justice. The king bestows prosperous and bountiful conditions upon land and people; thus the fertility of man, animals, and crops depends upon his acts. The king is a 'son of god'; he stands in an intimate relation with the high god of his people. If a first man is described in these terms, then he probably was thought of as a royal figure.

[15] Cf. on the primitive quality, M. Jastrow, who attempts to draw parallels with the figure of Enkidu in the Gilgamesh epic. Jastrow argues that Enkidu was originally a first-man form. *AJSL*, XV (1899), 193–214.

THE MYTH OF PARADISE AND THE FALL

Yahweh Elohim planted a garden in Eden from of old,[16] and he placed there the man, as well as the tree of life in the midst of the garden and the tree of knowledge of good and evil. Yahweh Elohim gave a command to the man, saying: 'From every tree of the garden you may surely eat; but from the tree of the knowledge of good and evil you may not eat, for in the time of your eating from it you must die.'

. . . .

The couple were naked, the man and his woman, but they were not ashamed.

Now the snake was the most clever of all the wild beasts. He said to the woman: 'Is it really so that Elohim told you not to eat from any tree of the garden?' The woman said to the snake: 'We may eat from the fruit of the trees of the garden, but from the fruit of the tree which is in the midst of the garden Elohim said, "You must not eat of it nor touch it, lest you die".' But the snake said to the woman: 'You will certainly not die, for Elohim is aware that at the time of your eating from it your eyes will be opened and you will become like gods, who are knowers of good and evil.' Then the woman saw that the tree was good for food and that it was a delight to the eyes and desirable to cause understanding, so she took of its fruit and ate and gave to her man who was with her, and he ate. Then the eyes of both of them were opened and they realized that they were naked. They sewed together the foliage of the fig tree and made for themselves loin cloths.

Then they heard the sound of Yahweh Elohim who was walking to and fro in the garden during the day's breeze. The man and his woman then hid from Yahweh Elohim in the trees of the garden. Yahweh Elohim called unto the man and said to him, 'Where are you?' And he said: 'I heard the sound of your walking in the garden, and I was afraid, since I was naked, and I hid.' And he said: 'Who told you that you were naked? Have you been eating of that tree from which I commanded you not to eat?' The man said: 'The woman whom you gave to be with me—she gave to me

---

[16] *Miqqedem*, once this verse is separated from the temporal statement in 2:4b–6, is probably to be understood as temporal, rather than spatial. It is used here, as often in Scripture, to set the time of a mythical or *heilsgeschichtliche* event; cf. Isa. 46:10; Pss. 74:12, 77:6, 12; Hab. 1:12; Mic. 5:1, and others.

from the tree and I ate.' Yahweh Elohim said to the woman: 'What is this you have done?' The woman replied, 'The snake beguiled me[17] and I ate.'

Then Yahweh Elohim said to the serpent: 'Because you have done this, you are more accursed than any animal or wild beast; on your belly you shall go and you shall eat dust all the days of your life.' Unto the woman he said: '[Because you have listened to the words of the serpent][18] in pain you shall bear offspring. You shall desire your husband and he shall rule over you.' To the man he said: 'Since you listened to the voice of your woman and ate from the tree which I had commanded you, saying, "Do not eat from it," cursed is the soil because of you. With hard toil you shall serve[19] it all the days of your life. By the sweat of your brow you shall eat food until your return unto the dust, for you are dust and unto dust shall you return.'[20]

Yahweh Elohim said: 'Behold, the man has become like one of us who know good and evil. Now, lest he stretch forth his hand and take also from the tree of life and eat and live forever'—he drove out the man. And he placed eastward[21] of the garden of Eden the cherubim and the flaming sword, which would move this way and that, to guard the way to the tree of life.

This myth explains the harshness of existent reality in the face of a god who wills good for man. Here man is now in command of a wisdom which enables him to exist independently of God's

---

[17] *Naš'a* may mean leading astray from the correct path as well as leading astray with false information; cf. Isa. 19:13; Obad. 3; the Qere of Ps. 55:16; and possibly II Chron. 32:15, where *naš'a* is in parallelism with *sut,* 'to allure'. 'To beguile' is preferable in our text over the usual reading, 'to deceive', if the new knowledge of good and evil acquired by the couple is to be taken seriously.

[18] Some such introduction to this curse must be assumed. Most likely it has been displaced by the confused first sentence of the present curse, 'I will greatly increase your pain and your conceptions,' a sentence we have deleted from the above translation as a later addition.

[19] Emending *'akal* to *'abad;* cf. Budde, *Paradiesesgeschichte,* p. 67.

[20] This reading is very conjectural. The sentence upon the man is difficult; additions to the original text have almost assuredly been made. Verse 18 is omitted as an addition; it seems unrelated to the close parallelism in 17 and 19*a*. Verse 19*aγ* and 19*b* seem to have added elements that cannot be easily separated. The above conjecture omits 'for from it you were taken' as an addition of the final editor and emends *'adamah* to *'apar* in 19*a* to harmonize better with 19*b*. For a justification of the conjecture cf. my thesis 'Adamic Christology of Paul', pp. 391f.

[21] Or 'in front of'; cf. Humbert, *Études,* p. 16.

care.[22] Yet he dies like any other animal;[23] he lives a sweaty existence upon an unyielding soil. His women regularly go through the anguishing cycle of childbirth. Man himself has turned from God and attempted to order and control life by powers which he has seized. The primary cause for man's present predicament is in fact his refusal to remain under God's guidance. His sin is a serious disobedience, punished severely by a resolute god.

The man in the myth of paradise is strikingly different from his counterpart in the myth of creation. True, both are mortal, although the paradise myth gives a haunting glimpse of a possible immortality. There the similarity ends. The man of the paradise myth is without knowledge. Yet while he knows nothing, and in this sense can be compared with the child's life before the age of reason, he is not at all innocent of selfish or personal motivation. There is no acceptance of Yahweh's good intentions in a childlike manner. The excuses offered by both man and woman indicate that the fear of Yahweh referred to in 3:10 is the fear of getting caught and punished; it is not awe or contrition. When the opportunity to free himself from the yoke of the god presents itself, the man is eager to have the chance to create his own destiny, even though it be a destiny separated from the deity. Thus the situation of the man is one of ignorance without innocence, naïveté without selflessness. As a result of his act of disobedience, the man himself has changed only in his acquisition of a new knowledge. The other changes occur in his environment. Death is now his unalterable future; hard labor on the ground, his only chance to live; the pain of childbirth, the necessary outcome of the awareness and desire of sex.

[22] The use here of good (*tob*) and evil (*r'a*) as antonyms to describe the tree of knowledge is similar to the appearance of the same antonyms in oracles, blessings, and curses (e.g., I Kings 22:1–28; Jer. 42:1–17, 21:1–10; Num. 22–24; II Sam. 14:1–20; Gen. 24:50, and others). The knowledge gained by eating the fruit is that wisdom and power which enable one to discern events, present and future, indeed to influence these events. To control the world belongs to the gods, and man's seizure of part of this control makes him like the divine beings. The myth has in mind the irruption of magic, wizardry, and all independent disposing over God's world. For a detailed discussion cf. my 'Adamic Christology of Paul,' Appendix C.

[23] The vexing problem of the tree of life cannot be discussed here. It must suffice to suggest that Gen. 3:22 must be taken seriously, not ironically. Had man been able to eat from the tree of life, he would have possessed an immortality which the gods would have been powerless to take away. Since he did not eat, he was and remains mortal. The story must suggest, therefore, that man once had the possibility of living forever. Cf. also Humbert, *Études*, p. 149.

THE COMPOSITE MYTH OF THE YAHWIST

What is the result when two stories, so contradictory in nature, are joined? According to Humbert the theology of the paradise myth conquers.[24] The joy of the goodness of creation and of Yahweh's benevolence has been partially submerged by the horror of the action of the first couple and the resultant punishments which afflict man's life. Yet the presence of the creation myth is not unimportant. The goodness of Yahweh is now more apparent, and his punishment of the man just, a punishment which in the paradise myth is almost an arbitrary, jealous act. One result of the combination is less fortunate. While the joining of the myths causes the union of two complementary theories of the divine, it also causes juxtaposition of two contradictory theories of the human. Some features of the man remain the same as in the original myths. He is mortal, made from the soil and the breath of Yahweh. But several characteristics have been changed or obscured by the union of the stories.

1. Man's original destiny is essentially no longer the fructifying of woman and soil. His role becomes the more passive one of remaining under Yahweh's guidance in the paradisal garden. The roles of procreation and labor become instead punishments, and the negative, painful side of these roles is stressed.

2. The intuitive acceptance of sex is dimmed by the paradise story. By removing the name 'Eve' (*hawwah*) and description of the first procreation to a time after the sin, express mention of the *use* of sex does not occur until its knowledge has been gained through the fruit of the forbidden tree.

3. There is now a before and an after in man's attitude toward the world and the deity. The paradise story gives no hint that man has a positive or faithful attitude toward God's acts. The first provocation brings the first disobedience. The creation myth, however, adds warmth and acceptance to the original character of the man. He responds positively to God's acts of creation and rejoices in the woman. This makes man before the act of disobedience a man who has accepted the goodness of the creator, and his disobedience becomes more reprehensible than ever because of the change in attitude.

[24] *Études*, pp. 66–81.

C

4. What is now least clear is the state of man's knowledge before his sin. The naming of the animals and woman belies the ignorance and naïveté assumed by the paradise story. Through the joining of the myths wisdom has become a created good, not an acquired evil. Thus the advance in discernment through the eating of the tree of knowledge becomes less pronounced. This in turn tends to place the emphasis more upon the act of disobedience and Yahweh's punishment as the main result of the sin.

The function and type of the man in the composite myth remains essentially that in the paradise story. He causes, not blessings and life, but pain, death, and enmity with God. His role as primeval king is thus almost completely submerged. He is now a man created for honor but who instead risks this honor for an autonomy which, in the final form of the myth, is at best an uncertain good, a man who causes a severance of community with God and the beginning of the evils of present life. Yet despite the seriousness of the sin, no concept of 'original sin' is to be found. The man brings death and introduces sin, but nothing is said about a change in man's nature which is passed on to his offspring.

The creation and paradise myths are clearly old traditions which must stem from the second millenium B.C. Thus Carl Kraeling's thesis that the theology which takes a serious and stern view of the first man is considerably older in the Hebraic tradition than that which takes an optimistic and ennobling view cannot be accepted.[25] Kraeling thinks that only with the exile (Ezek. 28) does the thought of an exalted first man appear. On the contrary, from the very beginning both an exalted first man and a man who brings sin and death were known. This awareness should put one on guard against the dangerous prejudgment that any exalted first man appearing in Judaism must be an importation from foreign cults.

The Priestly Traditions of the First Man

While a few other first-man traditions appear outside of Genesis, none of these is significant for our study.[26] The priestly

[25] Carl Kraeling, *Anthropos and Son of Man* (New York, 1927), pp. 151–53.
[26] The two most important passages are Ezek. 28:11–19 and Job 15:7f. The passage in Ezek. is almost despairingly difficult of interpretation, not only because of the possibility of textual corruption, but also—and mainly—because of the different levels of reference present. The prophet is speaking to a specific

traditions in Gen. 1:26–30 and 5:1–5 are, however, important both for Old Testament thought and as a source of later Jewish theology of the original man. Gen. 5 is almost surely older than Gen. 1.[27] Comparison with Gen. 6:9 and 10:1 indicates that Adam in 5:1a must be a proper name. Verse 5:1b describes how Adam was begotten, just as the rest of the chapter describes how other men were begotten: 'He made him in the likeness of God.' Verse 3 continues in this same direction. In verse 2, however, the singular pronoun gives way to the plural; male and female are described. Nothing, however, prohibits one from seeing in this verse reference to a first couple; it may actually be a later insertion under the influence of Gen. 1.[28] Thus verses 1–5 prove that the priests had accepted the myth of the first man, Adam. There are certain indications that, just as do the older traditions, Gen. 1 also thinks of a first couple.

> Then God said, 'Let us make man in our image, after our likeness; and let them have dominion over the fish of the sea, and over the birds of the air, and over the cattle, and over all the earth, and over every creeping thing that creeps upon the earth.' So God created man in his own image, in the image of God he created him; male and female he created them. And God blessed them, and God said to them, 'Be fruitful and multiply, and fill the earth and subdue it; and have dominion over the fish of the sea and over the birds of the air, and over every living thing that moves upon the earth.' (Gen. 1:26–28).

Nothing definite can be determined by the use of *'adam* itself in these verses. Here we find a profusion of uses, *'adam, ha-'adam,*

---

historical situation, using allusions to the king ideology of the Near East, and probably referring to a first man myth (although this does not seem to me quite as obvious as it does to some scholars). If such a mythic allusion is present, the story concerns a divine cherub created to serve the garden of Eden, located on the mount of the gods. The cherub lives in the favor of the gods until he sins, at which time he is cast out of the garden to the earth and is dishonored.

While the author of Job appears to be familiar with Gen. 2f., his allusion to a first man in Job 15:7f. has no relation to the former. This first man is wise and was created before the earth was fashioned. Certain similarities with Prov. 8 suggest that the Wisdom school had or was developing its own tradition about primordial events.

[27] Von Rad, *Genesis* (Philadelphia, 1961), p. 68.
[28] Cf. J. Skinner, *Genesis* (New York, 1910), p. 130.

with singular and plural suffixes referring to the human(s) created
by God. The words *zakar* and *neqebah*, 'male and female', are
often taken to be generic and thus to indicate that man as species
is being described. These words, however, are not commonly used
in a collective sense without the adjective *kol*.[29] In verse 28 God
blesses the humans and commands them to 'be fruitful, multiply,
and fill the earth'. If mankind in general is considered to be
created in Gen. 1, this command would be redundant. Gen. 5
describes in fact how the fulfilling of this commandment took
place. The simplest and most consistent interpretation of priestly
thought is that it assumes the creation of a single couple, a couple
which was known to the tradition through the creation and paradise
myth of the Yahwist.

What is the nature of this couple? Man is created in the image
of the gods. In Gen. 1:26 *'elohim* speaks to his council, 'Let us
make man in our image, according to our likeness'. The model
for man is *'elohim*, yet this probably means here not Yahweh
himself but the gods who make up his council.[30] The majority of
exegetes agree that *selem* means a plastic, material image.[31] Man
has a physical or 'corporeal resemblance'[32] to the gods; just as the
deities possess bodily form, so man is stamped with this form.
Whether or not *selem* includes the powers and spiritual qualities
of the gods is not as certain. It is at least true that P separates man
from the world more than from the *'elohim*. Man is an exalted,
honored being, and no trace can be seen of the first couple's
erring from the path God sets for them. They are blessed by the
creator and live a long and honorable life.

What is the function of the first man? Clearly it is to rule over
the created order, the animals and the earth. 'Let us make man
in our image, according to our likeness, and let them rule.' The
function of rulership is expressed also in 1:28 through the word
kabaš (to subdue). R. B. Y. Scott is perhaps correct in linking the
command in Gen. 1 to the onslaught of the divine forces against
those of chaos, which are always threatening to gain the upper

[29] E.g., Gen. 34:25; Lev. 6:11, 22; Num. 1:2, 20, 22; Judges 21:11; I Kings
11:15, 16.
[30] Cf. Ps. 8 and von Rad, *Theology*, I, 145.
[31] Among others, Humbert, *Études*, pp. 151–75: E. Jacob, *Theology of the
Old Testament* (New York, 1958), p. 167; L. Kohler, *ThZ*, IV (1948), 16–22;
von Rad, *Theology*, I, 144f.; Skinner, *Genesis*, p. 32.
[32] Skinner, p. 32.

hand.[33] In respect to the animals man is ruler. In respect to the earth, as it represents the remnant of chaotic force, he is its conqueror. Is Adam then thought of as the primeval king?[34] At this point a qualification must be added to the judgment expressed above that P accepts the tradition of a primeval first couple. Though the priests think in terms of such a couple, these mythic figures were of little importance to them as such. God assigns them the task of ruling, not so much because they are the first couple, but because they represent mankind or, perhaps more specifically, Israel. The priests are not concerned with political kingship, but they do picture man as king of creation. Thus, although the traits of kingship are present, it is misleading to say that P thinks of Adam as *the* primeval king. Just as the image of 'elohim is passed on through human procreation (Gen. 5:3), so man's function as ruler continues throughout the generations. The couple are also channels of fertility. 'Be fruitful and multiply, and fill the earth' runs the first commandment to Adam, a commandment which is at the same time a blessing. Insuring the fertility of man is, of course, another royal function, but again it is not bestowed here upon a unique king who is to give it to his people through the gifts of the tree of life, but upon mankind, represented by the first couple, as a gift of nature and of God's grace.

The first couple are thus to rule, to subdue, to procreate. These are all functions of the deity which are, nevertheless, given to man because he is the image of God. The similarity between the function of Gen. 1 and that of the creation myth in Gen. 2 is apparent. The difference is that in Gen. 2 the role is given to a concrete primeval man, who is a royal figure. In Gen. 1 the function is assigned to the first couple, mainly because they represent all their descendants. The anthropology of P could be described as the 'kingship of all men'. In distinction from the Jahwist, however, P says nothing about Adam's sin nor anything about Abel or Cain. The rulership which Adam possesses is

[33] From a conversation with Professor Scott. Many passages in the Old Testament imply that the *ṭehom* still exists and the idea of the continued threat of chaos is common in the thought of the Near East. Cf. Herbert May, *JBL*, LXXIV (1955), 9–22.

[34] As Bentzen and Engnell believe; cf. Bentzen, *King and Messiah* (London, 1955), p. 17, and Engnell's essay in *Wisdom in Israel and in the Ancient Near East*, ed. M. Noth (Leiden, 1955), p. 112.

passed through Seth to Abraham. If this suggests implicitly, as is very possible, that the first man is also the first Israelite (cf. also I Chron. 1:1), then P's anthropology would be, rather, the 'kingship of all Israel'.

Is There a 'New' Adam in the Old Testament?

Some scholars have argued that the reigning king in Old Testament thought is a representation of the primeval king; king ideology has been influenced by first man mythology.[35] If such an assertion were justified, then mythology of the original man would have a function within the 'messianic' theology of the Old Testament.[36] Corresponding to or contrasted with the first Adam (depending on how the first man was viewed) would be a 'new' Adam who would bestow blessings upon the historical order. As king ideology developed into futuristic messianism, the 'new' Adam would become an eschatological counterpart to the first. Such thought could then be considered at least a 'functional antecedent' of Paul's Adamic Christology,[37] if not a place to search for historical, that is, actual antecedents.

The difficulties in taking as valid the arguments for such a relationship stem both from insufficiency of evidence and from the doubtful methodological procedures often used. The similarity of motifs between king ideology and myths of the first man has often been used, as above, to prove that the first man is a king. If the origin of similar details seems to have its place within king ideology, then the researcher cannot reverse his argument to claim that the king is a re-presentation of the first man.

There *are* paradisal descriptions of the king's situation in the Old Testament.[38] Peace between animals and men, as it existed in Gen. 1, is to result through the agency of the king.[39] Mount Zion, the home of the king (cf. Ps. 2:6), is also the mythical mount of the gods (cf. Ps. 48:2). Yet in each case the motif can be shown to have its basic and original home in king ideology rather

[35] Cf. Widengren, *MRK*, pp. 174f.; Bentzen, *King and Messiah*, pp. 17, 41·
[36] I use 'messianic' here in a broad sense to include both the present as well as future (political-mythical) kings.
[37] That is, the function of the motif would be similar to the function of Paul's description of Christ as the Last Adam.
[38] Cf. Ps. 72; Isa. 9; 65:17–25.
[39] Cf. Isa. 11:6–9.

than in first-man mythology. The creation myth may very well lie behind some or all of the motifs, but as Mowinckel has convincingly shown, this relation proves that the king represents not the first man but rather the god himself.[40] The function of the king remains that of the function of the deity in creation, of bestowing fertility and bountiful conditions upon the created order. That Gen. 1 and 2 implicitly assign these functions to the first man means no more than that the man here is thought of in royal terms. Since king ideology does stem, at least in part, from the description of God's acts in the creation myths, there is indeed a relation between *Urzeit* and *Endzeit* in late Old Testament eschatology. First-man mythology, however, lies outside the main lines of relationship. It does not influence the royal theology and thus does not enter into messianic speculations.

The number of passages in the Old Testament which narrate or even allude to the myth of the original man are strikingly few. Yet the picture of Adam familiar to us as the bearer of sin and death is not the only image of the first man to be drawn from the Old Testament, and it may not even be the dominant one. The myth of creation used by the Yahwist, Job 15:7f., and, most importantly, the priestly materials, all portray the first man in honored and exalted terms. The myth of paradise used by the Yahwist, his final version in Gen. 2f., and the myth in Ezekiel are representatives of the more somber view. Not enough evidence exists, however, to judge decisively the relative popularity of either picture. It can only be said that when Adamic thought begins to flourish in the post-Old Testament period, neither view has excluded the other. In fact we may speculate that the myths did not arouse much reflection at all among the Old Testament writers. It remained for later Jewish and Christian theologians to raise the Adamic figure in importance, if not always in esteem.

[40] *He That Cometh* (Oxford, 1956), p. 81. Even Mowinckel seems misled by Isa. 11:6–8 into seeing a slight contact between messianism and the original king of paradise (cf. p. 182).

CHAPTER II

ADAM IN THE APOCRYPHA AND PSEUDEPIGRAPHA

The Old Testament writers bequeathed to their successors two separate uses of mythology about the first man. First, this mythology explains the fact of sin and the present predicament of the world. Secondly, it describes man's created state as intended by God. These same uses are developed in the post-Old Testament period, and the anthropological role of the myths grows even clearer. During this period Adamic motifs also begin to appear in eschatological materials, and a new role emerges. The description of Adam can now be the description of man's final, eschatological existence. Because of the close correspondence between *Urzeit* and *Endzeit*, the intended existence of man and his eschatological existence are essentially identical.

Before the investigation can begin, however, a methodological question must be raised. In what ways is an investigation of the Apocrypha and Pseudepigrapha useful in a study that has as its aim an understanding of Paul? If one admits only those materials which it is likely Paul actually read, then a chapter on the post-biblical writings would be of little value. Even of less value would be a chapter on rabbinic materials. Much of the Apocrypha and Pseudepigrapha is, as far as we know, contemporary or later than Paul, and as everyone knows, no written rabbinic materials existed until probably at least a century after Paul's death. Recent scholarship has increasingly been recognizing, however, that to seek out the literary background of a figure like Paul is not as important as recovering the general cultic and communal environment out of which he lived. On the one hand, the result is a few passages of uncertain worth, since one can rarely know with assurance what Paul actually read, once it is decided what he could have read. On the other hand, a rich religious culture is uncovered whose main concerns and ways of thinking Paul would undoubtedly have known. Particularly is the latter approach possible for the Jewish community, whose oral tradition one cannot doubt was both persistent and widespread throughout the centuries surrounding Paul. Philo's discussion of Adam proves, for example, that he knew rabbinic teaching of which we know nothing from rabbinic literature itself until later. Thus the task in this chapter is to seek out the main lines of Jewish thought, particularly those which are consistent throughout the period. For this purpose materials later than Paul are important, indeed even necessary, since one needs to know just which teachings the community found central enough to retain in its memory during the course of the centuries. Furthermore, it is necessary to know not only those ideas which Paul found congenial, and thus absorbed, but also those against which he reacted, and thus ignored. The significance of this insight for an understanding of Paul's Adamic Christology will become clear later. The following treatment of the materials in the Apocrypha and Pseudepigrapha is topical rather than historical; one should not forget, however, that diverse documents from different centuries are thus lumped together. As long as we are concerned about persistent, recurring themes, such an approach has no danger. A danger would arise, should some *specific* logion or detail witnessed only in a late writing be used to explain a *specific* Pauline passage. This I have steadfastly tried to avoid.[1]

Adam: *The Origin of Sin and Death*

Few writers with whom we are now concerned have so manipulated the Adamic myth that it serves for them only one

[1] Current scholarship rightly rejects a rigid boundary between apocalyptic and rabbinic thought; cf. W. D. Davies, 'The Jewish Background of the Teaching of Jesus: Apocalyptic and Pharisaism,' *ET*, LIX (1947/48), 233–37. D. Rössler attempts to make a sharp distinction between apocalyptic and rabbinic Jews in their attitude toward the law, but it is very doubtful whether he has made his case. Cf. his *Gesetz und Geschichte* (2d ed.; Neukirchen, 1962). By separating the material in this study, however, greater clarity will be gained, and in some cases rabbinic thought can be shown to depend upon, or be in the same community with, ideas found in the apocalyptic books. While the period this chapter covers ranges from perhaps the end of the second century B.C. (the date of Ben Sirach) until at least the end of the first century A.D. (IV Ezra and II Baruch), it is clear that speculation about Adam covers the entire period. Ben Sirach, the Wisdom of Solomon, Jubilees, some version of the Testaments of the Twelve Patriarchs, and most, if not all, of I Enoch, are pre-Pauline. L. S. A. Wells in Charles, *Apoc. and Pseud.*, II, 126f., dates the original bulk of the Adam books in the first century A.D., while Meyer in *RGG*, I, col. 91, dates the material even earlier. Charles dates II Enoch A.D. 1–50 (*Apod. and Pseud.*, II, 429), while Plöger suggests a date before A.D. 70 (*RGG*, III, col. 224). IV Ezra and II Baruch are usually placed at the end of the first century A.D., Plöger conjecturing around A.D. 100 for IV Ezra and from A.D. 70 to 132 for II Baruch (*RGG*, I, col. 902, and II, col. 699).

purpose. The fall of Adam can be described, yet at the same time the first man may be honored and perhaps partially exonerated of his deed. Nevertheless it is possible in most cases to discover the dominant motif, and an occasional writer is single-minded. Such is the case with IV Ezra. Surely the most intense statement of Adam as the first sinner occurs here. 'Thou didst lay upon him [Adam] one commandment of thine; but he transgressed it, and immediately thou didst appoint death for him and for his descendants' (3:7). This theme appears again and again; it reaches a climax in the anguished cry: 'O Adam, what have you done? For though it was you who sinned, the fall was not yours alone, but ours also who are your descendants' (7:118). Just this sentence illustrates a characteristic concern of the authors of this period: they are interested more in the results of Adam's deed than they are in Adam himself.

1. *Death.* Death is the most obvious effect of Adam's sin. Sirach sees death as a result of the warning in Gen. 2:17, 'You must surely die'.[2] Though Sirach 17:1f. might seem to indicate that death is a natural phenomenon, chap. 25:24, which blames Eve for the fall, conclusively indicates that death is, for the author, God's punishment, not man's natural state. 'From a woman sin had its beginning, and because of her we all die.' The same idea is implied by Apocalypsis Mosis 28. God refuses Adam's request to eat from the tree of life before he is cast out of the garden. The fruit may only be eaten at the resurrection. IV Ezra (3:7; 7:116–26) and II Baruch (17:3; 19:8, 23:4; 54:15; 56:6) continue the motif and indeed intensify it.[3]

2. *Corruption of Man's Situation in the World.* A second result of Adam's act is the distortion of that perfect world intended by God. In Genesis, man is beset by many evils as part of God's punishment. Sirach speaks similarly of the mental and spiritual anxiety which now lies as a 'heavy yoke . . . upon the sons of

---

[2] Sirach 14:17, though his Hebrew differs from the text of Genesis; cf. also 40:1 and 41:10.

[3] According to Charles, divergent strands of material embedded in II Baruch contain different ideas about death. Vss. 17:3, 19:8, and 23:4 acknowledge that death itself is the result of Adam's sin, while 54:15 and 56:6 speak only of premature death; cf. *Apoc. and Pseud.*, II, 475. Pfeiffer argues, I believe rightly, that Charles' attempt to isolate sources is not convincing; cf. *History of New Testament Times* (New York, 1949), p. 89. II Bar. teaches that both death and the brevity of life are results of Adam's sin.

Adam' (40:1–11). More commonly, all physical ills are traced to the first sin. In Apocalypsis Mosis God brings seventy-two 'strokes' upon Adam. 'The trouble of the first stroke is a pain of the eyes, the second stroke an affection of the hearing, and likewise in turn all the strokes shall befall thee' (8:2).[4] In II Baruch not only disease and mental anxiety but also erotic passion, murder, and moral turpitude have been caused by the sin of Adam.[5]

3. *Sin.* The third result of Adam's (or Eve's) deed is the cancerous growth of sin, which has now enveloped all humanity. This view is held by the earliest intertestamental writer,[6] but by the time of II Baruch and IV Ezra, the idea is proclaimed with an intensity unknown earlier. The major premise of most authors of this period is that sin is universal and every man is in fact a sinner.[7] As a rule these theologians make an effort to trace the universal presence of sin back to a cause. Yet while they may want to indicate which event introduced sin to man's history, they may not feel constrained to indicate how the cause and effect are linked together.[8]

For example Ben Sirach, while affirming the first couple as the first sinners, argues strongly for individual responsibility. Man cannot blame God, for He has neither desired sin nor commanded it to be.[9] Wisdom of Solomon appears to offer a novel solution for the problem of sin and death when it suggests that death is only apparent for the righteous (since their souls are immortal) while real for the wicked.[10] The book connects sin and death in such a way that it implies only he who sins really dies. While the author

---

[4] Cf. also Vita Adae 34:2.
[5] II Bar. 56:6. Cf. also 56:8ff.; IV Ezra 7:11ff.; Jub. 3:28; Apoc. Mosis 24.
[6] Cf. Sirach 25:24.
[7] That certain individuals were considered to be sinless does not alter the practical conclusion respecting mankind as a whole.
[8] E.g. the sin of the angels (Gen. 6:1–3). According to several books, the angels, by their illegitimate union with women, brought sin into the world; cf. T. Reuben 5; II En. 18; II Bar. 56:10; esp. I En. 9f., 64f., 86–88. None of the treatments of this motif, however, attempt to show just how this sin is transmitted throughout history. Occasionally it seems to be suggested that sin spread through the knowledge given by the angels to men, a knowledge not intended for men; cf. I En. 9 and 64f.; II En. 18. Still it is clear that no necessity resides in the spreading of this knowledge, so the motif cannot be taken as a serious attempt to provide a description of the inevitable transmission of sin.
[9] Cf. Sirach 15:11–15. Man's freedom is limited, however, in areas other than moral decision.
[10] Wisd. 2:23–3:3. Cf. also 1:13–16, where it is godless men who have 'summoned death'.

alludes to the story of Adam, neither this nor any other event is the single cause of sin, and thus of death. Each man brings death upon himself. The clearest example of a theology which maintains both the importance of Adam in the history of sin and yet the individual's entire responsibility occurs in II Baruch. 'For though Adam first sinned and brought untimely death upon all, yet of those who were born from him each one of them has prepared for his own soul torment to come, and again each one of them has chosen for himself glories to come . . . . Adam is therefore not the cause, save only of his own soul, but each of us has been the Adam of his own soul' (54:15, 19).

Since the book of IV Ezra differs from all other pseudepigraphal writings in its view of the origin of sin, it cannot be discussed here in detail. The author has so defined the causal relation between Adam's sin and the sins of his offspring that his formulation has sometimes been called a doctrine of original sin.[11] By his sin Adam has brought about a change in his inner nature, a change passed on to his offspring.[12] Nevertheless IV Ezra still clings to an affirmation of the *possibility* that man may overcome his inclination to sin. What separates the author from most Jewish thought is the pessimistic tone which is ever present in the apocalypse.[13]

For the above writers Adam functions as an explanation of the serious condition (death, travail, sin) in which the world finds itself. Their main interest is not in creating a mythology or in writing a 'biography' of the first man. In so far as Adam is portrayed as a sinful being, his locus is squarely within Jewish theology about man, sin, and evil, although by contrast he could be related to the doctrines of creation or eschatology.

---

[11] So N. P. Williams, *The Ideas of the Fall and of Original Sin* (London, 1917), p. 79; F. R. Tennant, *The Sources of the Doctrines of the Fall and Original Sin* (Cambridge, 1903), p. 229; C. K. Barrett, *A Commentary on the Epistle to the Romans* ('H.N.T.C.'; New York, 1957), p. 111. I take the basic notion of a doctrine of original sin to be the assertion of an explicit connection between the event in the garden of Eden and the inclination to, and fact of, sin in every man. That is, the doctrine attempts to explain 'scientifically' just how Adam's sin has caused each man to be a sinner.

[12] E.g. 3:26; 4:30; 7:92, 116–26.

[13] The references to God's mercies in IV Ezra are always put in the mouth of Ezra, and the angel never confirms these hopes; rather he dashes them by stressing God's strict righteousness.

The Exalted Adam

In the Yahwist's narrative Abraham, not Adam, is the first father of Israel, while Israel is a counter-measure of Yahweh to overcome the disorder that has overtaken the world. The priestly materials implicitly revise some of this tradition. Adam, as God's image, passes down this image through Seth to Abraham. The first man has thus become the first Israelite. The shift is significant. When Adam is seen as the first patriarch, Israel itself becomes the main purpose of God's creation. Israel is no longer an attempt of Yahweh to re-create within history a good world; it is now the original creative purpose of God. What remained implicit in the Hebrew Bible now becomes explicit in later Jewish theology. Both in apocryphal and pseudepigraphal literature and in rabbinic theology Adam is often exalted and may play a role quite different from that of the bearer of sin and death. He becomes the image of the humanity God intended in creation, a humanity to be restored in the new creation. His role as first patriarch becomes clearly expressed.

When Adam is thus glorified, his function as death-bringer may be muted and the origin of sin ascribed to a different cause. In fact the literature of this period suggests several different explanations of the origin of sin besides Adam. Perhaps the easiest alternative was to lay the blame upon Eve.[14] A second scapegoat is Satan.[15] While still other solutions to the problem of sin and death can be found,[16] the greatest competitor to Adam is the myth based on the mingling of angels with the daughters of men (Gen. 6:1-3). This illicit act may simply appear as *a* cause of sin rather than *the* cause. Jubilees, for example, makes no great change in the Genesis narrative, but there does seem to be a subtle shift in emphasis. The tone of the writing shows that the times of great corruption begin with the desire of the angels.[17] II Enoch

---

[14] Cf. I En. 69; Sirach 25:24; II En. 30:18; 31:6; Vita Adae 3:2; Apoc. Mosis 8:2, 11.

[15] Vita Adae 12-16; Apoc. Mosis 16:3.

[16] The Qumran community, for example, fearlessly traced the origin of sin back to God's creative act. Cf. 1QS 3:13-4:26, where the Spirit of error is created by God and placed in man just as is the Spirit of truth. For a detailed treatment of this section see W. D. Davies, 'Paul and the Dead Sea Scrolls: Flesh and Spirit', in *The Scrolls and the New Testament*, ed. Krister Stendahl (New York, 1957), pp. 171-74. A different judgment is reached by F. Nötscher, *Zur theologischen Terminologie der Qumran Texte* (Bonn, 1956), p. 179.

[17] Jub. 3:27; 5:1-10.

describes the fallen angels, now in torment, and says that they 'befouled the earth with their deeds' (18:4f.). In I Enoch this popular myth is clearly used as a description of *the* origin of sin (chapters, 9f., 64f., 85–90). The theologian who exalted the first man was thus not taking a radical or heretical step. It was just as acceptable not to emphasize Adam's sin as it was to stress it, and the author of I Enoch is not liable to the charge of distorting tradition any more than is the author of IV Ezra.

ADAM AS THE FIRST FATHER OF ISRAEL

An early and clear case of the exaltation of Adam occurs in Ben Sirach 49:16, within the long section 44–49 (or perhaps to 50:24) which is a description of Israel's history.

No one like Enoch has been created on earth,
for he was taken up from the earth.
And no man like Joseph has been born,
and his bones cared for.
Shem and Seth were honored among men,
and Adam above every living being in the creation
[καὶ ὑπὲρ πᾶν ζῷον ἐν τῇ κτίσει 'Αδάμ].[18]

Here Adam is glorified above all men. But he is also the first patriarch, as the context suggests at several points. The heading of the section says that the praise is to be of 'Our Fathers'. In verse 16 Adam is linked with Shem and Seth, through whom the pure lineage of Israel was transmitted to Abraham.[19] Why then is Adam exalted? The answer must be because he is the first father of Israel. II Enoch also evidences this motif. Adam is a forefather, the first of Israel's race. This is implied in 33:10 and 58:1f. Enoch speaks of Adam as 'our father'. That means Adam is seen by the Jewish author as a father, since Enoch is certainly

---

[18]After an extended section which progresses through history to comparatively recent events, such a casual retreat to Adam is strange. Louis Ligier argues that Adam is placed out of context in order to show a relation between the first man and Onias, the high priest; cf. *Péché d'Adam et péché du monde* (Paris, 1960), pp. 314–18. Adam is thus the type of ideal man, and Onias as the bearer of salvation is seen as related to the ideal man. It should be noted that the Hebrew fragment of this section has a slightly different text from that underlying the Greek, reading: 'But above every living thing was the beauteous glory [*tip'eret*] of Adam.' Cf. *Apoc. and Pseud.*, I, 506 f.

[19] Cf. also I En. 60:8; Jub. 2:23.

assumed to be an honored patriarch. Here also Adam is glorified more than in any other similar treatise.[20]

Other examples of this motif could easily be given,[21] but I shall only note as a final instance the most striking one of all, to be found in I Enoch. In chapter 37 the lineage of Enoch through Seth to Adam is described. The importance of this lineage becomes clear in the dream vision (chapters 85–90). Adam appears under the imagery of a white bull. Nothing is said about his sin, and his descendants (through the lineage of Seth) are also described as bulls. In fact all the patriarchs are white bulls until Jacob, who (perhaps because of biblical imagery) appears as a white sheep.[22] Only at the end of days does the white bull reappear in the person of the Messiah. Then the redeemed people of his kingdom are changed into white bulls as well. Adam is thus both the first father and the image of eschatological humanity.

ADAM AS THE IMAGE OF AND PROMISE FOR ESCHATOLOGICAL HUMANITY

Adam is for writers throughout the entire period an honored patriarch. But the question now arises: Does the exaltation of Adam necessarily belong to his role as first patriarch, or may it indicate still another function? Adam could be the first father without possessing the extraordinary attributes he is sometimes given. In fact IV Ezra portrays a first father who is dishonored.

[20] Despite the author's awareness of the story of the fall (chaps. 31f.), the burden of guilt is placed on both the devil and Eve (30:18; 31:6). Adam is also promised the resurrection (32:1). However, one MS (labeled 'A' in Charles) places Adam and Eve in hell in 41:1f. The other, and shorter, MS used by Charles (called 'B') omits Adam and Eve from the number of people being tormented. Not only is MS B closer to the thought of II En. elsewhere concerning Adam, but it may also contain the earlier and more original text; so A. Vaillant, *Le Livre des secrets d'Hénoch* (Paris, 1952), pp. iv–v. Vaillant argues, however, that Charles's 'B' text is based on an inferior MS, and the one Vaillant believes best differs from Charles's in several respects. This difference is most notable at the end, where in Vaillant's text appears a long story about the miraculous birth of and prophecies about Melchizedek. Vaillant also argues that the entire II En. is Christian in origin. His evidence appears to me quite weak, however, with the possible exception of the Melchizedek passage, and this passage is not found in all MSS. For a brief discussion of the uncertainties about II En., cf. D. S. Russell, *The Method and Message of Jewish Apocalyptic* (Philadelphia, 1964), pp. 61f. It should be noted that II En. 30:18, 31:6, and 32:1, mentioned above, are not found in the text Vaillant accepts.

[21] Cf. Wisd. 10:1 within the section 10:1–11:20; Vita Adae 27:3; Apoc. Mosis 41:3; Jub. 19:24, on which see J. Jervell, *Imago Dei* (Göttingen, 1960), pp. 34f. Jervell also argues strongly (pp. 33f.) that IV Ez. assumes Adam to be the first patriarch; cf. IV Ez. 6:53, 56. Jervell is probably correct, even though no trace of an honoring of Adam can be found in the treatise.

[22] So Charles, *Apoc. and Pseud.*, II, 252. Cf. Pss. 74:1; 79:13; Jer. 23:1.

I believe the answer is that Adam's nature becomes for some writers a description of God's intent for man, an intention realized once in the person of Adam, to be consummated for all believers in the age to come. Adam is God's perfect man, that one instance in history in which was realized man's intended nature. Certainly some descriptions of his person are extravagant and fanciful. Nevertheless, the concepts which lie behind the exaggerations are to be taken seriously. Adam was created with a nature of plenitude and power. The fanciful descriptions often are attempts to sketch in the inevitable uncertainty about what this state of completeness really was, or should have been. In the face of his present, precarious existence, man wonders about what God originally created. But he wonders more about the future: what God has in store for the righteous in the new age. The new existence is clearly painted by Jewish theologians in terms of original existence.[23] One implication of this connection is that the world to come is not an afterthought in God's mind. It is rather the complete return to that which once actually existed.

As we have seen, the glorification of Adam is not a notion foreign to the Old Testament. While the Yahwist wants to explain how the world came to its present sorry state, Adam is nevertheless seen as originally a wise and kingly figure—certainly the highest term of honor the writer knew. The Priestly theologians emphasize more obviously the stature of Adam and his royal functions; yet it is clear that Gen. 1 is concerned more about 'man' than about Adam. The use of the Adamic myth to describe God's intent for *man* is thus found already in the Old Testament. The difference, however, between the descriptions of Adam in the Bible and in post-biblical literature immediately raises the question: How can a superhuman Adam portray God's intent for humanity?

While the differences may actually be more apparent than real, in so far as there is a difference its cause is to be found in the interrelation of Adamic motifs with descriptions of man's eschatological nature. For many apocalypticists, the world to come is no longer simply a human, messianic rule on earth in the old historical order. New ideas about the trans-historical world to come led to new ideas about eschatological anthropology; but if this anthropology is to be equated with God's original intent for man, then

---

[23] This has long been held. Cf. the classic study of Gunkel, *Schöpfung und Chaos in Urzeit und Endzeit* (Göttingen, 1895), esp. pp. 367–71.

Adam must have existed as the blessed will some day in the future. *Urzeit* does equal *Endzeit*, and the portrait of the former influences the description of the latter. Sometimes, however, the process is reversed. What is believed will exist in the eschaton is said to have existed in the *Urzeit*. Just this has happened in the case of Adam. Judaism in its hope for the future imbued eschatological nature with certain characteristics, and it is precisely these characteristics which have come to be applied to Adam.[24] From a theological standpoint this was certainly a wise move, for it safeguarded the doctrine of creation from threats either from a too pessimistic sense of the misery of this world or from an over-enthusiastic eschatological fervor.

In what ways, then, is Adam exalted? For one thing, he is frequently called a king, although there is rarely any elaboration upon the idea.[25] What the writers prefer to emphasize is the kingship of all men. Ben Sirach, who in 49:16 probably is thinking of Adam's kingship, transfers this characteristic to mankind in 17:1-14. How easily the kingship of Adam is convertible to that of man is also seen in Wisdom of Solomon, where in 9:1-3 the author speaks of man's rulership in more detail than he speaks of Adam's in 10:2. Adam as king functions in this literature (so also in Gen. 1) as a description of God's intent for man and as an affirmation of man's central place in the universe. Some sources imply that Adam lost his crown, while others suggest that man's royalty remains a permanent possession. IV Ezra, II Baruch 14-15, and Apocalypsis Mosis 24 witness to the loss. Ben Sirach and Wisdom of Solomon seem to suggest that the rulership still is manifested in man's dignity. In the one case, rulership belongs only to God's intent for man; in the other it is manifested, at least in a faded manner, in present existence. The motif of man's royalty plays no role in descriptions of man's eschatological nature.[26]

[24] There are, it must be acknowledged, certain limitations and confusions involved in the identification, since Adam must necessarily be pictured as living in the physical world. That the exalted Adam is always found in this physical order shows how little knowledge or interest the Jewish theologians had concerning a pre-existent, 'heavenly' Adam.

[25] Cf. Jub. 2:14; II En. 30:12; IV Ez. 6:53f.; Apoc. Mosis 24:4. Slav. Vita 34 seems to reject the idea.

[26] At best there are very weak undertones in I En. 90:30; Apoc. Mosis 39; Vita Adae 48; Rev. 3:21; 20:4; I Cor. 6:2f. Perhaps one reason for the reticence in elaborating upon *Adam's* kingship is just the difficulty of having this motif serve as a description of eschatological man.

D

A second way of exalting Adam is to say that he possessed glory (*kabod*). While glory primarily belongs to God in Jewish tradition, it can be given to men or angels, particularly to whoever stands in the presence of God's own glory and absorbs its brilliance. *Kabod* is not, of course, the essence of God; rather it is his 'appearance', his 'side-turned-toward-men'. But when applied to men, *kabod* comes close to denoting a super-human or super-corporeal existence. Adam's glory is clearly pictured in Apocalypsis Mosis. Eve was clothed with glory (identified here, however, with righteousness) and lost this clothing through her sin (ch. 20). When Adam suffers the same fate he exclaims, 'O wicked woman! What have I done to thee that thou has deprived me of the glory of God?' (21:6). Here the glory possessed by Adam is God's own glory. Later in this treatise God will promise that in the resurrection glory will be restored to Adam. The author of II Enoch, if the long text may be trusted, considers Adam to have been a creature, 'honorable, great, and glorious' (30:11).[27]

A difficult problem concerns the use of the phrase, *kol kabod 'adam*, 'all the glory of *'adam*', which appears several times in the Qumran material as a reference to eschatological glory.[28] Does *'adam* refer to mankind or to the first man?[29] Neither syntax nor context makes it certain which is correct, although the absence of any other allusions to Adamic mythology in the Qumran materials inclines me toward the former alternative. The issue is not, however, of great importance, for the anthropological thrust of the context remains the same regardless of which translation is accepted: the saints will inherit the glory which was intended for man from the beginning but which has yet to be consummated. Thus whether or not *'adam* is general or specific, Wernberg-Møller's judgment is correct: 'The glory in store for the pious is

---

[27] If *tip'eret* is the original reading in Sirach 49:16 (see note 18 above), this verse is another reference to the glorious nature of Adam. So esp. P. Wernberg-Møller, *The Manual of Discipline* (Leiden, 1957), p. 87, n. 80. Ligier is correct in seeing that for Sirach Adam is the revelation of man as he was intended to be in creation; cf. *Péché d'Adam*, pp. 318f.

[28] 1QS 4:23; CD 3:20; 1QH 17:15.

[29] Among the scholars who read 'Adam' are the following: O Cullmann, *Christology*, pp. 141f.; W. H. Brownlee, *BASOR, Supplementary Studies*, 10–12 (1951), as quoted and accepted by Davies, *Paul and Rabbinic Judaism* (2d ed.), pp. 356f.; Wernberg-Møller, *The Manual of Discipline*, pp. 27, 87, n. 80; G. Vermès, *Discovery in the Judean Desert* (New York, 1956), pp. 140, 161; E. Schweizer, 'Die Kirche als Leib Christi in den paulinischen Homologumena,' *ThL*, LXXXVI (1961), 166.

identical with, or of similar grandeur to, the glory of Adam in Paradise before the Fall.'[30]

Similar affirmations of glory are found in almost every apocryphal and pseudepigraphal writing. I need only refer to a few typical passages. In IV Ezra 8:51 Ezra is exhorted to ask about the 'glory of those who are like yourself'; the context makes it clear that Ezra is here the prototype of the righteous man of the future. II Baruch in several places speaks of the exceeding glory of those who will inherit the eschatological age.[31] Much the same thing appears in I Enoch; the saints in heaven are said to be glorious beings.[32]

The correlation between the nature attributed to Adam and that which the righteous will receive in the new age should be evident. Before his Fall Adam possessed a nature of glory. The saints will possess glory as a gift in the new age. But which of these concepts is prior to the other? This question is crucial for determining the function of Adam's glory. I believe that the prior concept is the eschatological glory. The theologians are not concerned seriously about Adam as a mythic personality but rather about the eschatological future of Israel. Adam is invested with the glory of the saints because the new man can only be the recreation of what once truly existed in the *Urzeit*. Adam becomes the symbol or portrait of true man. At the same time he is the hope for the future.

Still another way of exalting Adam is to relate him closely to the angels. In some writings he is given a rank above the angels. The most extreme case occurs in Vita 12–17 in an account of Satan's fall. The first man was worthy of the adoration of the angels because he was created in God's image; but since Satan and his company would not give this honor, God drove them away from heaven.[33] For a few writers, Adam's very nature is similar to that of the angels. He is called in the long version of II Enoch a 'second angel' (30:11). I Enoch elaborates upon the idea, although Adam is not explicitly mentioned. 'For men were created exactly like the angels, to the intent that they should continue pure and righteous, and death, which destroys everything, could not

[30] *The Manual of Discipline*, p. 87, n. 80. 1QS 4:6–8 also affirms a belief in man's eschatological glory.
[31] II Bar. 51; 54:15, 21; 15:8.
[32] I En. 39:9; 50:1; 58:2; 103:2f.
[33] Cf. also Apoc. Mosis 7:20; Vita Adae 4:2; 33; Jub. 3:15; II En. 30:14.

have taken hold of them' (69:11). This is an important text for it shows that both the purity and immortality of the angels is ascribed to God's original creation of man. Yet the basic point of the motif is missed if its relationship with eschatological thought is not seen. Man in the kingdom of God is to receive a nature similar to or even superior to that of the angels. The correlation between Adam's nature and eschatological anthropology is again too close to be overlooked. No texts speak of future humanity being served by angels. In heaven both men and angels serve God. What is clear, however, is that man's eschatological nature is to be like that of the angels. A striking passage occurs in II Baruch 51:10.

> For in the heights of that world shall they dwell,
> And they shall be made like unto the angels,
> And be made equal to the stars,
> And they shall be changed into every form they desire,
> From beauty into loveliness,
> And from light into the splendour of glory.[34]

I Enoch, which has ascribed angelic nature to original man, asserts that eschatological man also will have this same nature. According to chapter 104 the saints are to shine as lights of the heaven; they are to 'have great joy as the angels of heaven'; and they are to 'become companions of the hosts of heaven'. Certain similar phrases in the Qumran writings probably point to the same belief.[35] It is tempting, and perhaps valid, to add evidence from the New Testament. Paul believes that the righteous will judge the angels in the new age (I Cor. 6:2 f.). In reply to the riddle of the Sadducees, Jesus answers: 'Is not this why you are wrong, that you know neither the scriptures nor the power of God? For when they rise from the dead, they neither marry nor are given in marriage, but are like angels in heaven' (Mk. 12:24 f.). Both Adam and eschatological humanity are like the angels. The correlation suggests that Adam functions as a portrait of the new humanity. Even the exalted title of 'second angel' is nothing more than the ascription to Adam of that nature which all the righteous will receive in the last day.

---

[34] C. also II Bar. 51:12.

[35] 1QS 11:7f.; 1QH 3:22, 11:12. Cf. Nötscher, *Zur theologischen Terminologie der Qumran-Texte*, p. 149, and M. Mansoor, *The Thanksgiving Hymns* (Leiden, 1961), p. 117, notes 6 and 7.

The descriptions of Adam as a once exalted being given us in the Apocrypha and Pseudepigrapha have now been discussed.[36] I have tried to show that the main concern of the Jewish theologians is not to perpetuate or expand upon a traditional myth, though this was perhaps also an enjoyable pastime. Rather the Adamic myth serves the purpose of portraying Jewish anthropology. The correlation between Adam's nature and that of man in the world to come means that the figure of Adam has been decisively influenced, not by *Urmensch* speculation, but by ideas of the new humanity. Since what God has in store for man once actually existed in creation, the first man is invested with all those characteristics, in so far as they can be applied, which the theologians believed the new humanity would be given. All of these motifs are beautifully drawn together by the vision in I Enoch 85–90, which we have already discussed. Here the identity of original and final humanity is made explicit. Just as Adam as the first patriarch appears in the *Urzeit* as a white bull, so the righteous (i.e., Israel) are transformed at the eschaton into that same animal. The restoration of Adam's true humanity in the *Endzeit* could not more clearly be indicated.

Adam and Eschaton

The relationship that exists between the original nature of Adam and eschatological anthropology leads naturally to the question whether the theologians believed Adam would have a personal role in the eschatological events. Often this question has been answered in the affirmative.[37] I have tried to show, however, that man, not Adam, is the true subject of the Adamic motifs in the Apocrypha and Pseudepigrapha. In fact, Adam almost never is mentioned when eschatological happenings are being described.

Those writers who relate Adam to the presence of sin and death picture the new world as a reversal of the work of Adam. What is emphasized is the great contrast between present and future worlds.[38] Here Adam is not thought of as an actual figure in the *Endzeit*, nor, for that matter, is the Messiah usually said to play a direct role in the restoration. T. Levi 18:9–12a has some-

---

[36] But cf. Addendum I below.
[37] See Introduction.
[38] Cf. IV Ez. 7:119–26; 8:51–54; II Bar. 56:6 with 73:1–74:1.

times been used as evidence for a view which relates Adam to the Messiah.[39] True, in this passage the Messiah *is* said to be active in the events of the eschaton. Adam, however, is but a symbol for the righteous ones, the 'saints', and the implication is that Adam's deed is in sharp contrast to that of the Messiah. Furthermore, in view of the present uncertainty about the provenance of this particular section, to let it weigh too heavily in any conclusion about Jewish views is precarious.[40]

The relation of Adam to eschaton is quite different in the materials which use him as a description of God's intent for man. Here there is a parallelism rather than a contrast. Yet, again, the figure of Adam himself rarely appears and even then plays no independent role in the endtime events. For those thinkers who wish to correlate creation and salvation, the myth of Adam is important only as it can ensure the anthropological link between the two *kairoi*. The anthropology of creation is the anthropology of salvation. Nevertheless, salvation still belongs to Israel. This limitation is safeguarded in the myth by its claim that Adam was the first Israelite.

Twice Adam does have a personal role in the eschaton. One of these occurrences is no more than a passing reference.[41] The other shows just how interwoven are the motifs of Adam as patriarch and as promise for the new humanity and how subordinated is the personal figure of Adam to the community which relates itself to him. The promises God makes to Adam are the clue to the meaning of the Apocalypsis Mosis. In an early part of the book, Seth and Eve pray that God might grant Adam of the oil from the tree of life, so that Adam might recover from the illness that besets him. Michael answers Seth: 'Seth, man of God,

[39] See Introduction.

[40] Recent studies on the Testaments have made a certain judgment on the writing difficult. A relationship with Qumran seems likely; cf. A. Dupont-Sommer, 'Le Testament de Lévi (xvii–xviii) et la secte juive de l'Alliance,' *Semitica*, IV (1952), 33–53. On the other hand some scholars have recently argued that whatever *Urtext* lies behind the present MSS, the Testaments as we know them have been completely rewritten by Christians. Cf. the excellent discussion by M. de Jonge, *Novum Testamentum*, IV (1960) 182–235. De Jonge believes (pp. 205–208) that T. Levi 18 has been so completely redacted by Christian hands that it is impossible to recover the Jewish (Essene) *Urtext*.

[41] Cf. II En. 32:1: 'Earth thou art, and into the earth whence I took thee thou shalt go, and I will not ruin thee, but send thee whence I took thee. Then I can again take thee at My second coming.' The second coming is here the eschatological awakening. This passage does not appear in the shorter text.

weary not thyself with prayers and entreaties concerning the tree which floweth with oil to anoint thy father Adam. For it shall not be thine now, but in the end of the times. Then shall all flesh be raised up from Adam till that great day—all that shall be of the holy people. Then shall the delights of paradise be given to them and God shall be in their midst' (13:2–4). This first mention of the resurrection does not make clear who is the holy people or whether Adam is included.

The second reference occurs in Eve's description of the events which caused the expulsion from paradise (28:3f.). Here there is an explicit promise to Adam, on condition that he refrain from sin. But the next reference has no condition; Adam not only will achieve the resurrection but he will also be exceedingly glorified: 'I will transform thee to thy former glory, and set thee on the throne of thy deceiver' (39:2).[42] The final promise occurs virtually at the end of the book, certainly at the end of the real 'business' of the drama, where Adam has finally been buried in the earthly paradise. God speaks to the body of Adam one final time (presumably the soul is already residing in the heavenly paradise): 'I told thee (that) earth thou art and to earth shalt thou return. Again I promise to thee the Resurrection; I will raise thee up in the Resurrection with every man, who is of thy seed' (chap. 41).

Here lies the real message of hope of the whole book. Despite the distortion which has come into man's existence, according to the author largely because of Eve, the tension is resolved by God's definite promise of the resurrection life to the seed of Adam. Here it is certain that Adam functions as the father of Israel. Because Adam is assured of a resurrection, the Jewish reader can believe that he is assured of one also. The *assurance* depends upon Adam's place as the father of Israel. The *nature* of the new humanity depends upon Adam's primeval existence in glory. Thus even here the mythic role of Adam is subordinated to the anthropological function the motif serves. Adam rises because he is the first father of Israel, but what is crucial is that his seed will rise as well.

---

[42] The motif of the throne which is to belong to Adam cannot be taken to mean that Adam will have a role as judge in the new age, i.e., that Adam and Son of Man have been assimilated here. Satan as a once honored angel possessed a throne of glory or honor, which is to be given to Adam because he is the first patriarch. Nowhere in this literature does Adam ever have the function of judging mankind.

CHAPTER III

ADAM IN RABBINIC LITERATURE

The main motifs about Adam found in the apocryphal and pseudepigraphal writings recur consistently in rabbinic discussions. A study of the rabbis will thus serve to confirm the results of the previous chapter. As before, our aim is not primarily to seek out particular sayings Paul may have learned, but rather to discover the most significant uses of the Adamic myth within the rabbinic schools. The similarity of intertestamental with rabbinic theology suggests both that some contact existed between the two groups of thinkers and also that the motifs played a part in rabbinic theology from the earliest times. Since most of the authors of those rabbinic logia about Adam which have been preserved for us are later than the first century, it must on the other hand be admitted that often no proof exists of such a continuity. What can be demonstrated is that the majority of rabbis interested in Adam are Palestinian scholars of the third century or earlier.[1] If one couples apocryphal, pseudepigraphal, and rabbinic thought together, then it is fair to say that Jewish interest in Adam ran consistently high in Palestine from the first century B.C. through the third century A.D. After the third century, interest appears to have declined, at least in orthodox circles. Both temporally and geographically, Jewish Adamic thought centered in areas which were also those of the earliest church.

The Sin of Adam

The sin of Adam is an assumed fact for most rabbis, even for those who glorify his original nature. For example in one popular logion, Adam is created, placed in the garden of Eden, sins, and is

---

[1] Of a sampling of seventy-two rabbis in whose name rabbinic logia are given, thirty-one are Tannaim (nearly forty-five per cent of the total). Of the remaining, by far the greatest number are early Amoraim from the third century A.D. All told, fifty-seven of the seventy-two are no later than the third century. Of these seventy-two, fifty-eight, or eighty per cent, are Palestinian. Even when the Tannaim are subtracted, the Palestinian Amoraim still outnumber their Babylonian counterparts.

expelled all within the twelve hours of the sixth day of creation.[2]
Hence follows the cry of ben Pedaiah: 'Who shall uncover the dust
from your eyes, O Adam, for you were not able to stand in your
trials even for an hour and behold, your sons guard all the commands which were given to them, and abide in them.' The sin of
Adam is here understood as disobedience of the Torah. His
situation with respect to the Torah is made explicit in another
popular saying which affirms that Adam was placed in Eden to
busy himself with Torah and to keep its laws.[3] Some logia seem
intent on intensifying where possible the guilt of Adam.[4] Most of
the traditions which are concerned with Adam's fall are, however,
more interested in the results of the fall than they are in Adam
himself.

The Results of Adam's Sin

As is well known, the usual rabbinic view of sin is that it
stems from the evil impulse, the *yeṣer ha-r'a*. While IV Ezra
thinks Adam has caused the impulse to become part of man's
nature, the rabbis fearlessly traced its origin back to God's
creation.[5] Yet since man is able to overcome temptation, everyone
is responsible for his own sins. A typical story pictures righteous
men reproving Adam for having brought death to them. Adam
retorts: 'As for me, I have only one sin to my account, while in
your case there is not a single man among you who has not at least
four transgressions to his account!'[6] Accordingly only a faint
echo is heard of the apocryphal and pseudepigraphal belief that

[2] Transmitted anonymously in *Pesik. R.* XLVI (187*b*); *Pesik.*, p. 334;
P.R.E. 11; *ARN*, א, I (3*a*); *Lev. R.* XXIX, 1; ascribed to R. Levi (an early
Amora) in *Mid. Teh.* Ps. 92, sec. 3; to Judah b. Pedaiah (an early Amora) in
Tanh., šemini 8 (15*a*) and *Tanh. B., ber'ešit,* 25 (9*b*); and to Aha b. Hanina (an
Amora) in *Sanh.* 38*b*; cf. also *Gen. R.* XVIII.6.

[3] *Pesik.*, p. 202; *Sanh.* 56*b* (with some variants and additions); *P.R.E.*12;
Gen. R. XVI.5f. Parts of these traditions go back to the Tanna Judah b. Bathyra.
demonstrating the general antiquity of the motifs.

[4] Cf. *Tanh., šemini* 8 (15*a–b*); *Tanh. B., tazri'a* 11 (20*a*); *Pesik. R.* VII
(26*b*); *Gen. R.* XXII.13; *Num. R.* XIII.3.

[5] The subject has been treated fully by many scholars; cf. Davies, *Paul
and Rabbinic Judaism*, pp. 20–27; S. Schechter, *Some Aspects of Rabbinic
Theology* (New York, 1923), pp. 242–92; Tennant, *The Doctrines of the Fall and
Original Sin*, pp. 169–76; Williams, *The Ideas of the Fall and of Original Sin*,
pp. 60–72.

[6] Anonymous traditions in *Num. R.* XIX,18; trans. that of *Midrash Rabbah*,
eds. H. Freedman and M. Simon (London: Soncino Press, 1939), referred to
hereafter as Soncino trans.

Adam somehow caused the expansion of sin in the world.[7] As first sinner Adam functions rather as the cause of the physical corruption to which man and the world are now subject.

Above all, man's own existence is distorted. A popular tradition, apparently stemming in its basic form[8] from the third century, lists six things Adam lost because of his sin.

> All *toledoth* [generations] are defective, except two. Ruth 4:18 and Gen. 2:4. And why are they defective? R. Judan said in R. Abun's name [other traditions ascribe this to Reuben]: the six corresponds to the six things which were taken away from Adam, viz., his lustre, his immortality, his height, the fruit of the earth, the fruit of trees, and the luminaries. . . . R. Aibu said: His height was cut down and reduced to one hundred cubits. . . . R. Berekiah said in the name of R. Samuel b. Nahman: Though these things were created in their fulness, yet when Adam sinned they were spoiled, and they will not again return to their perfection until the son of Perez [viz. Messiah] comes. . . . Whence do we know it of his height? . . . R. Judan said: It indicates a height of one hundred cubits. R. Simeon said: Two hundred. R. Eleazar b. Simeon said: Three hundred. . . . R. Abbahu said: Nine hundred cubits.[9]

The number six is forced, being derived from the arithmetic value of the letter *waw*. At least some of the individual items enumerated in the list of six existed before the final logion was derived. All three of the attributes concerning man—lustre, life, and stature—seem to have had such a pre-history.[10] The kind of thinking represented by the logion is thus certainly Tannaitic.

[7] Cf. *Yeb.* 103b; *Shab.* 146a; *A.Z.* 5a–b, 22b.

[8] The early Amoraim Reuben and Shemuel b. Nahman.

[9] *Gen. R.* XII.6, Soncino trans.; parallels in *Num. R.* XIII.12 and *Tanh. B.*, ber'ešit 18 (6b–7a). The defective quality of the *toledoth* stems from the omission of a *waw* from the spelling except in the two instances enumerated. Since a *waw* has the numerical value of six, the rabbis are led to speculation about the number.

[10] Some sayings are Tannaitic; notice the Tannaim Simeon and Eleazar b. Simeon in the logion just quoted. The R. Judan who asserts a height of 100 cubits for man in the new age is not to be confused with the Judan (a 4th century Amora) at the beginning of the logion. He is rather Judah b. Ilai, a Tanna of the mid 2nd century; cf. *Num. R.* XIII.12 and *Sanh.* 100a. Cf. also *Exod. R.* XV.21, which contains a different list of lost attributes.

Here the new age is said to correspond to the original creation, while man deprived of these original gifts is man as he exists today. The story in its present form is confused, however, in its view of the stature of Adam. The rabbis depict different heights his restored body will possess: one hundred, two, three, and even nine hundred cubits. The figure of one hundred cubits, however, seems to have been the traditional size, at least during the Tannaitic period.[11] Thus Adam probably was thought to have had an original stature of one hundred cubits *before his sin*. The confusion arises because R. Aibu's (Abbahu's) statement is inserted into the discussion of Adam's height: Aibu, an Amora, interprets the reduction of Adam's stature as a diminution *to*, not from, one hundred cubits. Although his saying contradicts the context, the reason for the discrepancy is not hard to discern. An entirely separate tradition ascribes to Adam a tremendous size, a sprawling body which stretched from one end of the earth to the other and from the ground to the heavens.[12] What Aibu has in mind, apparently, is the reduction of Adam's size to one hundred cubits from this gigantic body. At any rate, the disparate traditions should not keep us from seeing that according to the basic statement in the rabbinic discussion, man originally possessed a size of one hundred cubits to which he will one day be restored. Thus the rabbis saw man's physical stature drastically reduced as a result of Adam's sin.[13]

Also lost to Adam was his brilliance, or glory (*kabod*). Judging from the number of references to the motif, the rabbis greatly delighted in describing this glory, as we shall see presently. According to most, Adam did not carry it with him out of Eden. Targum Jonathan tersely adds to Gen. 2:25 the words, 'But they did not tarry in their glory'. From a being of radiant splendor, the

[11] For Judah b. Ilai, see the previous note; so also the Tanna R. Meir in *Sanh.* 100a (a parallel in *B.B.* 75a); Judah's statement reappears in *Sanh.* 100a, but here it is based on a different argument from that in *Gen. R.* XII.6.

[12] Cf. *Gen. R.* VIII.1; for discussion see below.

[13] The reason size is considered a value is not clear from the context, but perhaps the meaning is that a larger man could more easily control his environment. If such is the case, the weakening of the abilities and faculties of Adam as a result of the fall is related to the loss of stature. According to the Tanna R. Simon, Adam once possessed great strength, now lost by sin (*Gen. R.* XVI.1). This original might, however, did enable Adam 'in the hour in which he was at peace with his creator' to open with one turn of his spade the four riverheads which went out from Eden. Cf. also *P.R.E.* 14.

image of God's own glory, Adam became the ordinary, weak human being every man now knows himself to be.

Most important, Adam brought to himself and thus to man the loss of life. Adam's death was not part of his own destiny. The famous Tanna R. Akiba says that Adam chose the path of death (*Gen. R.* XXI.5). According to R. Hanina, Adam was meant to be spared death, just as Elijah actually was.[14] The rabbis were most concerned, however, with the death of mankind. Here only a few examples need be given. R. Judah, a Tanna, interprets Deut. 32:32 to be addressed to Israel and to mean: 'You are sons of Adam who brought death upon you and upon all his descendants coming after him until the end of all generations.'[15] Even Moses, in those traditions where he is considered sinless, dies because of the sin of Adam.[16] The point is that death is caused by God's *decree* upon all mankind because of Adam's misdeed. Thus death comes both to the sinful and the sinless.

Yet there is a view which claims that death is not imposed on all men regardless of their moral state but rather is a penalty for actual sin.[17] This argument usually takes one of two forms: (a) if all men die, it is because all men sin;[18] or (b) in fact there have been certain men who did not die, and this must mean they did not sin.[19] The disagreement is at least once brought into open conflict in Amoraic times (*Shab.* 55a-b). R. Ammi lays down the strict doctrine that there is no death without sin nor any suffering without iniquity. A logion of the Tanna Simeon b. Eliezer is brought out in support of Ammi; the logion claims that even Moses and Aaron died through their own sin. But objections to this view are raised, and the final judgment of the Talmud is that Ammi's view had successfully been refuted. The basic and ultimate judgment of Jewish theologians is that death is God's decree upon all men because of Adam.

The repercussions of Adam's sin were not limited to man's nature itself. Just as did the Yahwist, some rabbis attributed the

[14] *Gen. R.* XXI.5. Hanina is probably the early Amora.
[15] *Sifre Deut.*, sec. 323 (138b). For other examples cf. *Gen. R.* XVI.6 and XXI.1.
[16] *Deut. R.* IX.8; parallels in *Eccles. R.* VII.13.1; *Koh. Z.* VII.13; usually this saying is ascribed to R. Levi.
[17] This divergence of opinion among the rabbis has also been seen by A. Marmorstein, 'Paulus und die Rabbinen,' *ZNW*, XXX (1931), 271.
[18] Anonymously in *Num. R.* XIX.18; *Tanh. B., ber'ešiṭ,* 29 (11a).
[19] R. Judah in *Pesik.,* p. 152.

difficulties in man's battle with environment to Adam's act. A Tanna, R. Nathan, said: 'Three entered into judgment but four came out cursed. Adam, Eve, and the serpent entered into judgment, but the earth was punished with them' (j*Kil.* I.7, 27*b*). The losses most frequently mentioned are those of the earth's fertility and the original light in the sky. Trees and plants once bore immediately without the need of human labor.[20] God originally created a great light or lights to shine in the world. The removal of this light was one of the penalties attendant upon Adam's sin and expulsion from the garden.[21]

Finally, a few passages imply that as a result of the first sin a breach in man's relationship with God has been opened. According to one tradition, Adam experienced a change in the sound of the *baṭ qol* (the divine voice) after his sin.[22] Before he sinned, the *baṭ qol* was a gentle voice; afterwards, Adam heard only a harsh sound. The Tanna Simeon b. Yohai argues that before his sin Adam had the confidence to stand on his feet without flinching when he listened to God; afterward, when hearing the voice, he hid (*Num. R.* XI.3). Even worse, once out of Eden Adam reviled and blasphemed God.[23] He now both hated and feared God. Some logia go even further, though how seriously these are to be taken is not always clear. Several are early Amoraic traditions found in *Sanhedrin* 38*b*. According to Rab, Adam was a *min* (heretic), who turned his heart from the true worship. R. Isaac argues that Adam attempted to disguise the circumcision with which he was created. Nahman thinks that Adam denied God (the fundamental principle).[24] The first man in these sayings is quite clearly the prototype of the anti-religious man, whether Gentile or apostate Jew. Because of Adam's sin irreligion becomes reality

---

[20] Cf., e.g., *Gen. R.* X.4 and *Exod. R.* XV.21.

[21] A popular and early tradition. Cf. *Gen. R.* XI.2 and XII.6; *Lev. R.* XI.7; *Num. R.* XIII.5; j*Ber.* VIII, 12*b*; *Pesik. R.* XXIII (118*a*); *Tanh.*, *šemini* 9 (16*b*); *Haq.* 12*a*. The saying is attributed to various authors, including the Tannaim Eleazar and Simon. A. Altmann has argued that the motif of the light is gnostically derived; cf. 'Gnostic Themes in Rabbinic Cosmology,' *Essays in Honour of the Very Rev. Dr. J. H. Hertz* (London, 1942), eds. I. Epstein, E. Levine, and C. Roth, pp. 28–32. The possible origins of a motif, however, cannot be allowed to determine its function in its present context.

[22] *Pesik.*, p. 83, by the Tanna R. Ishmael; a parallel in *Num. R.* XI.3 assigns the saying to R. Abin, an Amora.

[23] So Resh Laqish, an early Amora, *Pesik. R.* VII (26*b*); parallels in *Tanh. B.*, *ber'ešiṭ* 25 (9*b*), and *Num. R.* XIII.3.

[24] Cf. also *ARN*, ב, I (2*a*).

for Adam and a possibility for every man. Thus not only man's physical life has been disrupted by Adam; his spiritual life is also threatened.

The rabbis, of course, maintained that Sinai had restored a proper relationship between God and Israel through the mediatorship of Torah.[25] This explains the relative paucity of sayings which speak of Adam's moral or religious attitudes after his sin. Only with respect to his 'being unto death' is the Jew similar to Adam. For this very reason the rabbinic tradition about Adam is not *primarily* a vehicle for the discussion of ethical values.

Adam the Exalted Father of Israel

Rabbinic theologians continued, and indeed expanded upon, the view that Adam was an honored father of Israel. Although the details the rabbis introduced into the mythology often differ widely from those found in the Apocrypha and Pseudepigrapha, the function is essentially the same. Here too it seems unnecessary to look to gnostic thought for essential clues to the meaning of Jewish theology, even though certain details may be most easily explained as coming ultimately from such mythology.

The question must again first be asked whether and in what ways rabbinic scholars avoided assessing Adam an unbearable burden of guilt. As was the case with the apocryphal and pseudepigraphal literature, the blame is sometimes transferred to Eve. A *baraitha*, giving the reasons for the Torah requirements concerning woman, implies that Eve is guilty of the first sin.[26] Adam was the first-born of the world and Eve spilled his blood; thus she (woman) was given the laws concerning *niddah*, blood at menstruation. Adam was the *hallah* of the world and Eve made him impure; thus, the requirement of the *hallah*, the separation of the dough. Adam was the light of the world (or of God) and Eve extinguished him; thus, the lighting of the Sabbath lamps. According to Simon b. Yohai (or Rabbi) Adam is like a man who commands his wife to use everything he owns except one jar. She promptly opens this jar and is bitten by a scorpion. When her husband comes home he divorces her (*ARN*, א, I, 3*b*). Some rabbis

---

[25] Cf. here Jervell, *Imago Dei*, pp. 91f.
[26] *Tanh. B.*, *noah* I (14*a–b*), *mesor'a* 17 (27*a*); j*Shab.* II, 5*b*.

understood the sin of the garden to be sexual in character, thus implying Eve was to bear the blame for the fall.[27]

Other theologians, while not blunting the guilt of Adam, did find it possible to provide him with a pardon and to picture him as worthy of God's forgiveness. In *Gen. R.* XXI.7 the report is given of a Tannaitic controversy as to whether God judged Adam in strict justice or with mercy, such that he could participate in the world to come. The dispute in the Midrash is not settled or harmonized, but the frequency of other allusions to Adam's pardon makes it clear that God's leniency was the usually accepted judgment. For example, the Tanna R. Eliezer teaches that Adam was created on *Rosh ha-Shanah* (*Lev. R.* XXIX. 1). At the twelfth hour he received a pardon. This is a sign to his descendants who will also go out from *Rosh ha-Shanah* with pardons. Thus Adam is here a type of the future Israelite on New Year's day.[28] There are, in addition, a few sayings which specifically carry on the old pseudepigraphal notion of Adam's repentance and fasting. A *baraitha* reports that Adam, who feared the world was slipping back into chaos, when the sun set at the end of the first Sabbath, wept and fasted all night (*A.Z.* 8a). The *Pirke de Rabbi Eliezer*, which has more than one parallel to the Pseudepigrapha's treatment of the first man, tells of Adam's fasting for seven weeks in the Gihon River.[29] Several sayings mention that Adam at various times offered sacrifices.[30] That these ideas are old is proved by a statement of R. Meir, who draws together several details into one logion. 'Adam was a great saint [*ḥasid gadol*]. When he saw that through him death was ordained as a punishment he spent a hundred and thirty years in fasting, severed connection with his wife for a hundred and thirty years, and wore clothes of fig [leaves] on his body for a hundred and thirty years.'[31]

Thus according to some rabbis Adam came out from the garden of Eden with a pardon—free from the burden and guilt of his deeds. While many of the logia are not primarily concerned to portray an exonerated Adam, such a view is implied. Particularly

[27] Cf. the *baraitha* in *Sot.* 9a–b; *Gen. R.* XX.4; *P.R.E.* 13, 21; *ARN,* א, I (2b); *Targ. Jon.* to Gen. 4:1.
[28] For other examples cf. *ARN,* א, I (4b); ב, VIII (12a); *P.R.E.* 19, 20; *Pesik. R.* XL (167a–b), XLVI (187b–88a); *Mid. Teh.* Ps. 92, sec. 3.
[29] *P.R.E.* 20; cf. Vita Adae 4–8; Slav. Vita 35–39.
[30] *P.R.E.* 31; *A.Z.* 8a; Targ. to Ps. 69:32; *ARN,* א, I (4a); *Shab.* 28b.
[31] *Erub.* 18b; trans. that of *The Babylonian Talmud,* ed. I. Epstein.

does the exoneration become clear when these sayings are contrasted with those portraying a rebellious and blasphemous Adam. The first man can now more easily become the first father of Israel.

A further step in the direction of claiming Adam for Israel is taken by some traditions which, so far from picturing a guilty Adam who needs pardon, number him rather among the righteous. The statement of R. Meir has just been noted: Adam was a great saint. One discussion among the rabbis concerns the naming of the city, *qiryaṭ-'arbʻa* (Gen. 23:2), taken to mean the 'City of Four'. Of several interpretations, perhaps the most popular is that the city is the burial place of four couples, Adam, Abraham, Isaac, Jacob, and their wives.[32] How Adam is related to this city is uncertain; for us the crucial point is that he is listed among the patriarchs. One appearance of this saying adds the judgment that these were 'four righteous men' (*Gen. R.* LVIII.4). Once Adam is seen as righteous, however, his connection with the penalty of death becomes problematical. The issue is explicitly treated at least once, in a saying of the Amora R. Hama b. Hanina. 'Adam was worthy not to have to taste death.'[33] The reason God brought death to Adam was that he foresaw the attempts of Nebuchadrezzar and Hiram to make themselves gods. Ezekiel 28.13 is here interpreted to mean: 'You [Hiram] are the one who brought death to the one in Eden.' A further saying by the Amora R. Berekiah supports that of R. Hama.

The above materials indicate that these rabbis tended in varying degrees to remove from Adam his guilt and any unsavory character he may have acquired. What is important to note is not the particular means of removing this guilt but the fact that it was both possible and helpful to do so. While differences exist between rabbinic tradition and apocryphal and pseudepigraphal literature with respect to the means, the fact of such a removal is clear in both instances, and we may query now whether the reason for the removal of guilt is also similar.

---

[32] Thus R. Isaac, an early Amora; *Erub.* 53a; *P.R.E.* 20; *Gen. R.* LVIII.4; *Sot.* 13a.

[33] *Gen. R.* IX.5; a partial parallel in *B.B.* 75a–b.

ADAM AS THE FIRST PATRIARCH

1. *Adam as the beginning of Israel's destiny*. The rabbis appropriated Adam for the history of Israel in several ways. The motif to be discussed here suggests how Adam is related to all human history and therefore to its destiny. Yet the real history and destiny described becomes that of Israel. While Adam is still a lifeless mass stretched out before God, he is shown all future generations and their acts.[34] According to one important and popular variation God shows Adam only the righteous, or the leaders of Israel, who will descend from him.[35] The implication is that the true descendants of Adam are the righteous ones, that is, Israel.

Closely related to the above motif is the discussion about a book of Adam.[36] The history of the world is written down before it occurs and is shown to Adam. Related also is the statement, quoted in the name of R. Johanan, an early Amora, that all souls were created in the garden of Eden on the sixth day of creation and were, apparently, bonded to the covenant at Mt. Sinai, וכולן היו במתן תורה.[37] The relation of the souls to Sinai again suggests that the people really in mind here are the Israelites.

One thing is clear. So far there is no suggestion or hint that Adam himself has anything to do with determining these destinies. It is God who decides the status of man and works out his salvation in history. What is left to man, says *Midrash Tanhuma* in its version of the motif, is man's decision for good or evil, a teaching at least as old as Ben Sirach.[38] Adam is passive; he sees what is to be, but God does the ordaining and God solemnly affirms that not one thing shall be altered. I know of only one logion which is an exception. According to the Amora R. Jose b. Hanina, the verse of Jeremiah 2:6, 'Through a land that no one passed through and

---

[34] *ARN*, א, XXXI (46a); *Sanh.* 38b; *A.Z.* 5a; *Mid. Teh.* Ps. 139, sec. 6; *Tanh. B.*, ber'ešit 28 (11a); *Gen. R.* XXIV.2. Though several authorities are cited for this tradition, the original apparently goes back to Eleazar b. Azariah, a second generation Tanna.

[35] The idea goes back to the Amora R. Judah b. R. Simon, *Gen. R.* XXIV.2; *Exod. R.* XL.3; *Pesik. R.* XXIII (115a); *ARN*, א, XXXI (48a).

[36] *Gen. R.* XXIV.1–5; *Exod. R.* XL.2; *Pesik. R.* XXIII (115a); *Mid. Teh.* Ps. 139, sec. 6; *Eccles. R.* 1.6. The notion is difficult to date; it probably is no later than the 3rd century, cf. *Gen. R.* XXIV.5 (Jacob of Kefar Hanan) and *Eccles. R.* I 6 (where it is stated with some doubt that R. Johanan, an early Amora, might be the originator).

[37] *Tanh, pequdi* 3 (133a).

[38] Ibid.; cf. Ben Sirach 15:14–17; 33:10–13.

E

where no man dwelt', alludes to a decree of Adam (*Ber.* 31*a*). The first man had the prerogative to decree which lands would be inhabited and which would not. Only this passage, of questionable importance since it stands alone, suggests in any way that Adam is the determiner of destinies. Thus the meaning of this motif is not that Adam determines or becomes the fate of mankind.[39] The materials are concerned rather with the rabbinic notion of God's foreknowledge and predestination. Man's external history is firmly in the hands of God. Only his moral choice remains free. Yet God foreknows that the right choice will be made by successive generations of righteous Israelites. Just at this point the motif becomes a doctrine of assurance. Man need never ultimately despair, because the world will be sustained by God's grace and the righteous response of Israel. Thus according to R. Eliezer the days shown to Adam are days of salvation for Israel such as the Exodus and Sinai.[40] God's mercies to Israel begin with Adam; the future course of this mercy and the effects it has on the true descendants are disclosed to the patriarch.[41]

2. *Adam as hasid.* Certain isolated traditions picture Adam as performing pious acts or as being in what was for the rabbis a normative relationship with God—normative, that is, for Israel. Some of these we have already considered.[42] In addition Adam is said to have been a writer of psalms, certainly at least of Psalm 139.[43] One of the main duties of Adam was to praise God below as the angels praised him above (*P.R.E.* 12). Adam along with the angels sang the opening verses of Psalm 92 in praise of God and the Sabbath.[44] Relevant here is also the popular motif that Adam was put in the garden to study and obey certain parts of Torah, to 'busy himself with words of Torah'.[45] Just as Israel was later to be, so Adam in the beginning was in a Torah relation to God. Many traditions exist which argue over the particular commandments assigned to the first man; often these are consid-

---

[39] The notion of all souls being *in* Adam only occurs once, to my knowledge; cf. *Exod. R.* XL.3.

[40] *Tanh. B., ber'ešit* 28 (11*a*).

[41] So also Jervell, *Imago Dei,* p. 106.

[42] *Erub.* 18*b*; *A.Z.* 8*a*.

[43] *B.B.* 14*b*; *Mid. Teh.* Ps. 1, sec. 6, here ascribed to Nehemiah, and Ps. 139, sec. 2, ascribed to Judah, both Tannaim.

[44] E.g., Targ. to Ps. 92:1; *Mid. Teh.* Ps. 92, sec. 3; *ARN,* א, I (4*a*); the tradition goes back to Simon b. Yohai.

[45] *P.R.E.* 12; *Tanh. B., ber'ešit* 25 (10*a*).

ered to have been the so-called Noachic laws.[46] Finally the anonymous logion should be recalled which pictures the righteous at death confronting Adam; against their complaint he argues that he has disobeyed only one commandment, while even the best of the righteous have disobeyed at least four (*Num. R.* XIX. 18).

Taken together these sayings picture Adam performing religious acts which were later performed by Israel: Torah obedience, fasting, acts of repentance, the writing and singing of psalms of praise. The point does not rest upon Adam's perfect fulfilment of these acts but rather upon his acceptance of these as his duty. Of course Adam sinned at least once, but he did take as his normative relation to God that which was considered exemplary by rabbinic pietism.

3. *Adam as priest.* A few traditions not only show Adam making a sacrifice but also claim him as high priest in a line which descends to Jacob and Moses. A *baraitha* describes how Adam sacrificed an ox in gratitude for the sight of the sun on the morning of the eighth day.[47] This basic motif seems to underlie other logia. One such asserts that Adam offered a sacrifice of an ox whose horns were created prior to his hoofs (based on Psalm 69:32).[48] More startling is the assertion that Adam was clothed in the garments of the high priest. In *Tanhuma Buber* the question is asked: 'What were the tunics of skin with which God clothed Adam?' The answer is that they were garments of the high priest, for Adam was 'in the glory of the world'.[49] Since a *baraitha* held it permissible for the first-born son to exercise the priestly prerogatives before the tabernacle was established, it was, the text proclaims, permissible for Adam to be clothed in the high priestly garments as the 'first-born of the world'. But why does Adam wear the high priestly robe, since the *baraitha* speaks of the first-born offering sacrifice only as a priest, not as a high priest? The probable answer is given in the conclusion: Adam transmitted these robes through his first-born offspring (counting Seth as

---

[46] At basis a Tannaitic motif. Cf. *Gen. R.* XVI.6; *Num. R.* XIV.12; *Deut. R.* II. 25; *Song of Songs R.* I.2.5; *Sanh.* 56b; *Pesik.*, p. 202.

[47] *A.Z.* 8a; *ARN*, א, I (4a); cf. also the idea that Adam was commanded to sacrifice, *Gen. R.* XVI.5.

[48] *Hul.* 60a; *Shab.* 28b; Targ. to Ps. 69:32; *A.Z.* 8a. The psalm text lists horns before hoofs.

[49] *Tanh. B. toledot* 12 (67a), an Amoraic tradition.

first-born) to Jacob. Adam is the high priest because he is seen as
direct ancestor of Jacob, the father of Israel. Another tradition in
essence makes the same point as the above. R. Levi argues that
the staff of Moses was created at dusk on the sixth day and given
to Adam (*P.R.E.*40). Adam then handed down the staff to later
patriarchs (not the first-born, however) and by a devious process
Moses obtained it in Egypt. Though the staff is not specifically a
priestly symbol, it probably serves the same general function.
Moses was honored as a priest among the rabbis and the staff
was his symbol of authority.

The details in these stories are certainly not all intended to be
taken seriously. What is serious is the assertion of a continuity
between God's creation and the call of Israel. Just as the study of
Torah was commanded in the garden, so the possibility of sacrifice
existed from the foundation of the world as a means of relating
man to God. The mediatorships of Torah and cult were prepared
from the beginning and served to preserve mankind before Israel
met God at Sinai. Adam and the patriarchs were able to use them
because in some sense the early fathers *were* Israel and transmitted
(*masar*) these means to the Nation. Adam as a *ḥasid* and as a
priest, indeed the high priest, is so because he is seen as the first
patriarch of Israel.

4. *Adam as a father of Israel.* In the following logia Adam is
appropriated for Israel by being specifically related to the people
or the patriarchs.[50] In one *baraitha* Moses upbraids the Israelites
in the wilderness as being ungrateful people stemming from an
ungrateful ancestor (*A.Z.* 5*a–b*). Targum Jerushalmi to Gen.
3:22 adds to the biblical text the statement that many nations will
arise from Adam and in particular a great nation that will be able
to distinguish between good and evil. Another *baraitha* interprets
the flaming sword in Gen. 3:24 to refer to the Torah. This implies,
says the *baraitha*, that Adam at first refrained from intercourse
because he saw future generations going to Gehinna (*Gen. R.*
XXI.9). When, however, he understood that, in the future,
Israel would accept the Torah, he began to produce descendants.
Similarly in another place God is addressed: 'As you acquitted
him [Adam], you will acquit his sons in the future,' clearly bringing

[50] This position is argued strongly now by Jervell; cf. *Imago Dei*, pp. 102–
106.

Adam and Israel into the closest connection (*Pesik. R.* XL, 167*a–b*). Adam and Israel are again related in the form of a parable by the Amora Judah b. Simon (*Num. R.* XIII.2). A king, angry with his wife, drove her away. Later when he wished to recall her, she demanded a favor before she would return. So God drove Adam away, then later wished to recall Israel. The new favor Israel requests is God's presence in the Temple. The obvious implication is that Israel and Adam are seen as one, just as the woman driven out and the woman restored are the same.[51]

According to *Midrash Tehillim* Adam was one of thirteen patriarchs who were born circumcised.[52] In several other logia Adam is expressly linked with the patriarchs. The most popular of these traditions, already discussed above, puts the burial place of Adam and Eve in the cave of Macpelah, where biblical tradition had placed the graves of Abraham, Isaac, and Jacob.[53] In an anonymous tradition in *Baba Bathra* 14*b* Adam is called an 'elder' and included in the list of other patriarchs. An anonymous tradition in *Sukkah* 52*b* interprets the seven shepherds of Micah 5:4 as referring to seven religious leaders: David in the middle; Adam, Seth, and Methuselah on his right; Abraham, Jacob, and Moses on his left. The likeness of God which Adam bore is also seen in another tradition as being passed down to worthy Israelites (*B.M.* 84*a*). Here the beauty of various rabbis is said to be a reflection of the likeness of Adam. Whatever else may be implied in this saying, the point for us is clearly that Adam is the *Urbild* for the immediate ancestor of the nation. Once this logion follows an interesting haggadic tale about the Tanna R. Bana'ah (*B.B.* 58*a*). Bana'ah went to mark out at Macpelah the caves of the patriarchs. He came to that of Abraham and surveyed it. But when he arrived at Adam's a *baṭ qol* deterred him with the words: 'You have seen the image [דמות] of my likeness [יונק], but you may not see my likeness [יונק] itself.' A comparison with various people follows. Sarah was greater than all people who came after her. Eve was that much greater than Sarah. Adam was that much greater than Eve, and the Shekinah was that much greater than

---

[51] Cf. also *Sifre Deut.* sec. 323.

[52] *Mid. Teh.* Ps. 9, sec. 7; also *ARN*, א, II (6*b*). The idea of Adam's circumcision is also mentioned in *Sanh.* 38*b* and *Gen. R.* XI.6.

[53] Cf. Gen. 49:30f. *P.R.E.* 20, 36; *Erub.* 53*a*; *Sot.* 13*a*; *B.B.* 58*a*; *Gen. R.* LVIII.4.

Adam. This story says not only that Adam is the *Urbild* for Israel but also that he is the *Abbild* of God (*via* the Shekinah).[54]

To summarize: Adam is a follower of Torah; he is *ḥasiḏ* and priest; he is the ancestor of Israel; he is honored among the early patriarchs. When taken as a group all these passages become impressive witness that, according to one rabbinic view, Adam was appropriated and honored as the first patriarch. Whether asserted implicitly or explicitly, seriously or fancifully, the crucial point is the fact that Adam is seen in this way. This is not to suggest that the rabbis were agreed upon the view, nor even that a majority of them would have accepted it. What is clear is that such a position was at least known in many rabbinic circles from very early times.

The Exalted Nature of Adam

Of all the rabbinic reflections upon Adam, by far the most popular appear to have been those which spoke of his nature before the fall. Here occur the greatest variety of topics, the most fertile outpourings of imagination, the most repetitions of favorite logia.

1. *Adam as king*. This old motif is still honored by a few rabbis although most of the original intensity and meaning is gone. According to *Aboth de Rabbi Nathan* God made Adam to be king over the world, but the serpent wished to kill Adam so he could become king instead (א, I, 3*a*, 4*a*). R. Judah b. R. Simon (an early Amora) asserts in *Gen. R.* XIX.4 that that which is created later rules over that created earlier. So Adam, who was created last, is king over all the creation. The rabbi is reported in another source as saying that God intended Adam to be king below just as He was king above.[55] These examples suggest that the motif of kingship is used just as in Gen. 1 to speak of man's priority over all the created order.[56]

---

[54] These are two of the very few places where the motif of Adam as image of God is explicitly mentioned. Jervell's otherwise excellent chapter on the rabbis (pp. 71–121) is misleading to the extent that he groups and interprets much material which *can* be related to the image motif but which actually was not, as a general rule, so related by the rabbis. This is not to suggest that Jervell misinterprets the content that he includes but that he imposes upon the content a structure that the rabbis did not assume.

[55] *Pesik. R.*, Appendix (192*a–b*).

[56] For other examples cf. *Sanh.* 38*a*; *P.R.E.* 12; *Gen. R.* XXV.2.

2. *The wisdom of Adam.* Here is another traditional motif which does not prove of central interest among the rabbis. To my knowledge, only two logia are specifically concerned with the wisdom of Adam. The more prominent of these proclaims the superiority of Adam's wisdom over that of the angels.[57] Usually this logion appears in two parts. The first is a *pešer* on Ecclesiastes 8:1, which is interpreted as referring to Adam. In the second part the angels, who show a surprising amount of animosity toward man throughout many Adamic materials, quarrel with God over man's creation. God retorts that Adam's wisdom will be greater than theirs. He brings the animals before the angels, but they are unable to know what the names are. Adam, on the other hand, not only knows the correct names for all the animals, he knows also what his own name is, and even the name of God.[58] The second logion is pure fancy. Adam, as God's vice-regent, finishes the work of creation by making fire and by bringing the donkey and horse together to beget the mule.[59]

3. *Adam's relation to the angels.* The rabbis were more interested in the apocryphal and pseudepigraphal tradition that Adam was closely related to angelic nature. Several logia ascribe identity or similarity with the ministering angels. One of the earliest is based upon Gen. 3:22. Modern translations read thus: 'Behold, the man has become as one of us.' R. Huna, an Amora, however, reads, 'Behold the man *was* as one of us' (*Gen. R.* XXI.2). Adam before his sin and punishment was of similar nature to the divine world, but afterwards his nature was changed. This haggadah is very ancient. 'One of us,' according to R. Pappas (a first century Tanna) means, 'Like one of the ministering angels'. R. Akiba objects, but R. Judah b. Simon, arguing by an analogy (a *qezerah šewah*) between Gen. 3:22 and Deuteronomy 6:4, says the phrase means, 'Like the Unique One Himself'. The rabbis—the general view— argue that the phrase means, 'Like Gabriel', arguing from Ezek. 9:2.[60] The nature of the similarity

---

[57] *Gen. R.* XVII.4, here ascribed to the Amora, R. Aha; *Tanh. B.*, ḥuqat 17 (57b); *Pesik.*, pp. 60f., 66; *P.R.E.* 13; *ARN*, ב, VIII (12a); *Num. R.* XIX.3; *Eccles. R.* VIII.1.2.

[58] Whether this name is Adonai or YHWH is difficult to decide. Either could be justified from the context.

[59] *Pes.* 54a, a tradition by the Tanna, R. Jose; there are partial parallels in *Gen. R.* XI.2, XII.6, and LXXXII.14; cf. also *Targ. Onk.* to Gen. 3:22.

[60] All of this in *Gen. R.* XXI.5; cf. also XXI.2,4. Soncino trans.

is not spelled out, but the immortality which the angels enjoy is certainly one thing in the mind of the rabbis. *Gen. R.* XXI.4 explains that this similarity lay in the strength to live forever—a strength now taken away from Adam. A similar idea is credited to the name of the Amora R. Tanhuma; God created Adam to be like the ministering angels, to live and exist like them.[61] To be included here are also those traditions which describe the angels' ministry and/or praise of Adam.[62]

The function of these motifs is similar to those in the apocryphal and pseudepigraphal literature. The rabbis take as their starting point God's intent for man; man was to be immortal, righteous, the pinnacle of creation. His was a nature, however, which could be sustained only by a free decision for God. Adam sinned, that is, decided against God, to attempt to become himself a god,[63] and thus his exalted nature was lost by virtue of that decision. This intended nature will yet be given to man (this time as a gift, cf. *Gen. R.* XIV.8), and Gen. 3:22 in that new age will then be read: 'Behold let the man become as one of us,' or 'Behold the man has (now) become as one of us' (*Gen. R.* XXI.1, 7). Quite clearly the rabbis are not seriously concerned about Adam as a unique, never-to-be repeated form. It is only because Adam is the example of what man is to become that in these contexts he proves a popular figure.

4. *The glory of Adam.* Continued and much developed was also the motif of Adam's great glory. The imagination of the rabbis runs riot here, and the brilliance sometimes given the first man is almost beyond conception. That Adam did have a countenance or coat of glory was generally accepted throughout the entire rabbinic period. Simon b. Menasya, a Tanna, claims that the ball of Adam's heel outshone the sun. How much more, then, his face.[64] He adds that the purpose of the sun was to serve Adam, while that of Adam was to serve God. Man in his intended state was, on the one hand, the pinnacle of nature and, on the other, a fitting vessel for the praise of God. In an interesting

---

[61] *Pesik. R.*, Appendix (192*a*); cf. I En. 69:11, which is quite similar in idea.

[62] Cf. *P.R.E.* 19; *Tanh., pequḍi* 3 (134*a*); *Gen. R.* VIII.10; *ARN*, א, I (3*a*); *Sanh.* 59*b*. Many of these traditions are Tannaitic.

[63] Cf. here *ARN*, ב, I (3*b*).

[64] *Tanh. B., ḥuqaṭ* 17 (57*b*); *Lev. R.* XX.2; *Eccles. R.* VIII.1.2; cf. also *B.B.* 58*a*.

reversal of motif, the Tanna R. Simon, rather than suggesting that the Sabbath served Adam, argues that God sanctified the Sabbath by the shining countenance of Adam.[65] According to R. Meir, the coats of Gen. 3:21 were 'coats of light', אור, not 'of skin', עור, as the actual text reads.[66] Thus there was little dispute about the fact that Adam did have God's glory as part of his created nature, just as the theologians of the Apocrypha and Pseudepigrapha asserted.

5. *The body of Adam.* As already suggested, two entirely separate traditions existed which commented on the physical size of Adam before his fall. One asserted that Adam was one hundred cubits high, a size that will be restored to him (that is, to man) in the age to come. Probably implied here as well is that the first man operated with a perfect strength and power now no longer possible. A second logion pictures Adam as of truly gigantic size.[67] The core of the logion reads: 'He [God] created him as a lifeless mass [*golem*] extending from one end of the world to the other. He created him filling the whole world.'[68] The idea is thus that Adam, before God breathed life into him, lay sprawled without form, filling everything that is now empty space between earth and heaven.[69]

Clearly this is a popular saying (and therefore meaningful) for the rabbis. Yet what this meaning is, what its function within Jewish theology, is most problematic. Its popularity cannot simply be due to the imaginative exegesis found here of Deut. 4:32 and Ps. 139:5. Nor can it have its basis in the idea of Adam as the unity of mankind, in whom all men inchoately exist. Only one occurrence of the logion concludes with a statement that all the earth's righteous stemmed from some particular part of the

---

[65] *Mek., baḥodeš* 7.
[66] *Gen. R.* XX.12. Examples could easily be multiplied from other Tannaitic sources.
[67] *Gen. R.* VIII.1; XIV.8; XIX.9; XXI.3; XXIV.2; *Exod. R.* XL.3; *Lev. R.* XVIII.2; *Hag.* 12a; *Sanh.* 38b; *Mid. Teh.* Ps. 139, sec. 5; *Pesik. R.* XXIII (115a); *P.R.E.* 11; *ARN,* ב, VIII (11b). That this notion was popular during late rabbinic times is obvious from the number of places it occurs. Yet it is an early tradition, going back to the Tanna, Eleazar b. Azariah.
[68] *Gen. R.* VIII.1; Soncino trans.
[69] The word *golem* can mean both a mass of material before some specific shape is given to it (like a lump of dough) as well as an embryo. Whether these two meanings can be distinguished and one preferred over the other in the logion is not clear from the context itself.

gigantic Adam (*Exod. R.* XL.3). The logion cannot be explained as a microcosmic motif, since there is no hint at all here that Adam is considered a world to himself. If anything, he appears as part of the larger cosmos, for he once existed as the 'middle region' between earth and heaven. N. P. Williams' argument that the aggrandizement of Adam was designed to accentuate the gravity of his fall is no more acceptable than the other conjectures.[70] The most popular explanation of the saying links its origin with extra-Jewish sources, a suggestion which usually means some form of gnostic or Gayomard myth.[71] This suggestion is perhaps correct,[72] but it hardly satisfies as a real explanation of the function of the myth as it stands in rabbinic materials. The story nowhere even hints at what are usually reputed to be the functions of the *Urmensch* in such myths, that is, cosmological or soteriological roles.

I must admit that no satisfactory solution from within the *theological* framework of Judaism seems possible. Perhaps the reason for the logion's popularity is to be sought rather in other areas, such as those of folklore or the insights of psychology. Perhaps the function is to extol an ancient ancestor, although there are no particular hints that the gigantic size is seen as praiseworthy. Or again, it is just possible that the saying serves to explain the spatial gap between earth and heaven. If *golem* carries the meaning of 'embryo', then perhaps the idea is that Adam is an embryo within the cosmos (and thus related to the notion of Mother Earth?). Whatever the reason may be, I think it is fair to say that

[70] *Ideas of the Fall*, p. 56. Williams is followed by Davies, *Paul and Rabbinic Judaism*, p. 45, and by C. K. Barrett, *From First Adam to Last* (New York, 1962), p. 7. Williams' view might well be true for two appearances of the logion, after which there follows an account of the reduction of Adam's size: 'But when he sinned, the Holy One, blessed be He, laid His hand upon him and diminished him,' *Hag.* 12a, *Sanh.* 38b, Soncino trans. Yet since only two of the thirteen occurrences listed in note 67 above have this addition, it cannot explain the basic motif.

[71] Cf. Murmelstein, *WZKM*, XXXV (1928), 257; Staerk, *Soter II*, p. 15; Bousset, *Hauptprobleme der Gnosis* (Göttingen, 1907), pp. 219f.; J. M. Creed, 'The Heavenly Man,' *JTS*, XXVI (1924/25), 119; Jervell, *Imago Dei*, p. 99.

[72] Here Jervell is right in opposing Quispel's view that the Jewish Adam is the *source* of the gnostic *Urmensch;* cf. *Imago Dei*, pp. 96f. The extreme difficulty in explaining the idea of the gigantic body from Jewish motifs perhaps proves the non-rabbinic origin of the myth. Jervell quickly admits, however, that the function is different for the rabbis than for the gnostics. For Quispel's argument, cf. 'Der gnostische Anthropos und die jüdische Tradition,' *Eranos Jahrbuch*, XXII (1953), 195–234.

the logion, for all its popularity, appears isolated from the main theological currents of rabbinic thought.[73]

Other motifs more directly relate to the exaltation of Adam's nature. One, Tannaitic in origin, proclaims that the dust used to create Adam was taken from the four corners of the world.[74] *Pirke de Rabbi Eliezer* understands this to mean that man's nature knows no geographical limitations. Since, however, the saying can appear without this explanation (e.g., *Sanh.* 38a), a question is again raised as to the original function of the motif. Following the logion in *Sanhedrin* is a tradition given in the name of Rab, which tells from what parts of the earth the dust was collected for specific limbs of Adam's body. His trunk came from Babylon; his head, from Israel; his limbs, from other lands; his private parts from Akra di Agma (an immoral city). Rab's statement, while certainly it does not belong to the original logion, may yet hint that the Tannaitic saying originally had a microcosmic intent. A more complete and explicit statement of Adam as microcosmos, also Tannaitic, occurs in *Pirke de Rabbi Eliezer*.[75]

To be separated from the above ideas is the motif which tells of Adam's creation either *from* the dust of the spot to be occupied later by the Temple or *in* this spot.[76] Adam is created in the navel of the earth, in the pure ground where the Temple is to be built. This act of God shows his abounding love for man. After Adam is removed from the garden he is returned to this spot, there to live out the remainder of his days. The garden, Mount Moriah,

---

[73]Another popular logion about Adam's nature with an uncertain *theological* function is that which makes him into an originally androgynous creature. The idea is apparently Amoraic and is found in *Gen. R.* VIII.1; *Ber.* 61a; *ARN*, א, I (4b); *Tanh., tazria* 1 (17a); two traditions in *Mid. Teh.* Ps. 139, sec. 5; *Lev. R.* XIV.1. The concept of the androgynos was well known in Greek society; the rabbis knew this concept from the Greeks and even appropriated the Greek word. That the idea was integrated early into a Jewish frame of reference is shown by the discussion of the androgynos in Mishnaic law (cf. *M. Bik.* I.5 and all of *Bik.* IV, which was originally part of the *Tosephta*). Here it is assumed that such a person may actually exist, and as the rabbis develop the notion with regard to Adam no esoteric meaning is involved. In this case I think it likely that the logion is closely tied to its exegetical basis, explaining Gen. 5:2 ('Male and female he created *them* and called *their* name Adam') in the light of Gen. 2, where Adam is created first.

[74] *P.R.E.* 11; *Tanh., pequḍi* 3 (134a); *Sanh.* 38a. Ascribed to R. Meir.

[75] By a Tanna, Jose the Galilean; cf. *P.R.E.* 31. although this section has probably been greatly expanded from its original form. To be compared here are the microcosmic sayings in the Pseudepigrapha; cf. II En. 30:8–10, 13; Sib. Oracles III. 24–26.

[76] Cf. *P.R.E.* 11, 12, 20.

and the Temple location are seen as the same place.[77] *Gen. R.* XIV.1 links the motif to the idea of *hallah*. Adam was the *hallah* of the world, taken from the very center of the earth. According to the early Amora, Samuel b. Nahman, Adam was created from the place of his atonement, for God said, 'Behold, I will create him from the place of his atonement, and may he endure.'[78]

These motifs suggest that Adam had a nature which is sanctified; he carried within himself some of the holiness which the altar has and some of the nearness to God which that suggests. Whether, however, this characteristic was lost by Adam or whether it inheres in all men (or only in Israel?) is not agreed upon. Eve's work of making impure the *hallah* suggests the former, but in other cases the implication seems to be that every man stands in this sanctification by virtue of his creation.

As far as Adam's physical body is concerned, the rabbis thus suggest several things. He was of large or gigantic size; he was created out of dust from the various places of the earth, or from the dust of the Temple spot; he was created at once both male and female. In general he was thus seen to be an honored and exalted creation. These motifs do not necessarily fit together nor can they be used to form a composite portrait. For instance, the motif of the gigantic Adam shows no sign of having anything to do, from a form-critical standpoint, with the idea of the *androgynos*. To suggest that most of the rabbis would have envisioned such a composite picture is an illegitimate inference. With some notable exceptions, I believe that the presuppositions operating here are closely related to those which lie behind other motifs of Adam's nature. The first man serves as a description of God's intent for man. Because of the universality of sin, man cannot look to himself in the present age to fathom such a nature. Rather he must look to that instance in the past in which God's creative goodness was as yet unhampered by man's rebellion.

Adam and Sinai

The above section leads naturally to a study of the relation between Adamic motifs and eschatology. Yet a prior question must be raised. Since the rabbis often tend toward a non-

[77] Cf. *Targ. Jon.* to Gen. 3:23.
[78] *Gen. R.* XIV.8; Soncino trans. For other examples cf. j*Naz.* VII. 2, 56*b*; j*Shab.* II, 5*b*.

eschatological view of the world, do they contrast the event of creation with that of Sinai, or Adam with Moses? Clearly in some general way Sinai presents a corrective to the way of the fall.[79] Jacob Jervell has recently argued more specifically that for the rabbis the image lost by Adam is restored as a *possibility* by the gift of the Torah.[80] That is, with the gift of the Torah man now is able to live in a correct relationship with God. In effect Jervell thinks the rabbis have in these contexts turned 'image' into an ethical concept. One difficulty with this argument, as Jervell himself acknowledges,[81] is that the word or words for 'image' rarely occur in the logia he cites. Thus the evidence offered is mostly of a general or tangential nature. It is true that according to some traditions God at Sinai recreates Israel into that perfect humanity once given to Adam. But just as Adam sinned and lost this nature, so Israel sins (specifically in the worship of the golden calf) and again loses the nature.[82] This means that Adam's original nature or image is no more a possibility *in this world* for the Jew after Sinai than it is for the heathen. The Torah is important, for by following it the Jew prepares himself to receive the image in the *world to come*. But the new nature always remains an eschatological gift, dependent upon (but not identical with) a life of Torah obedience. The fact is that no particular relationship or typology of Adam with Sinai is created by the rabbis because the two motifs serve different functions. While Sinai and Torah traditions explain how man is to live so that God will grant him eternal life, the Adamic-eschatological traditions describe this future gift and how it will come.

More popular among scholars than the attempt to relate the fall with Sinai has been the suggestion that a comparison or typology exists between Adam and Moses.[83] Yet even here, perhaps surprisingly, there seems not to be any significant amount of comparison.[84] At least this holds true for the earlier period of

---

[79] E.g., *Tanh.*, *šemini* 8 (15a–b); *Gen. R.* XIX.7; *Num. R.* XIII.2; *Song of Songs R.* V.1.1; *Shab.* 145b–46a; *A.Z.* 22b; *Yeb.* 103b.

[80] *Imago Dei*, pp. 91f.

[81] Ibid., p. 92.

[82] The clearest example is *Num. R.* XVI.24, which is at least partly Tannaitic. Cf. also *Lev. R.* XI. 3; *Mek.*, *baḥodeš* 9.75ff; *Exod. R.* XXXII. 1.

[83] Staerk, *Soter II*, pp. 50ff.; Murmelstein, *WZKM*, XXXVI (1929), 51ff.; J. Jeremias, *TWNT*, IV, 862, and Jervell, *Imago Dei*, p. 115.

[84] Cf. *Tanh.*, *šemini* 8 (14b), anonymous; *Shab.* 28b, R. Judah; *Deut. R.* IX. 8, R. Levy.

rabbinic theology; the most conclusive evidence cited by Murmelstein and Staerk is demonstrably late. Certainly the evidence hardly allows one to conclude[85] that Moses is an *Abbild* of Adam. The use of different figures in Israel's history in parallelism or contrast is a familiar technique of the rabbis and not every use of this method can be considered a genuine typology. The paucity of explicit comparisons of the two figures may be further evidence that traditions about Adam and traditions about Sinai are concerned about essentially separate values and categories.

Adam and Eschaton

Despite the sometimes grotesque and fantastic imagery used by the rabbis, these theologians were at heart sober-minded and even at times rationalistic. They did not follow the *via negativa*, but they did know that God was above all human comprehension. Likewise, the rabbis were aware of the limitations of human knowledge with respect to the world to come. The times of the Messiah might be very similar to present life, but the age of the resurrection could only be described in imperfect analogies.[86] This accepted limitation of human knowledge probably accounts for the hesitation of the rabbis to speak openly of the future life. They do talk about the new world, but when compared with similar sections of apocalyptic literature this reticence becomes quite apparent.[87]

One of the analogies they accepted was traditional: the time of the end will be similar to the time of the beginning. Probably this was even a prominent analogy. It is at least the case that the connection between the garden of Eden and future blessedness was popular. Indeed, *gan 'eden* has become the name for 'heaven', the abode of the blessed. At least in some sources the righteous dead are dwelling in the garden now.[88] It is here that God will dwell with the righteous in the world to come. The righteous are studying Torah in the garden; there God will prepare a banquet

[85]As does Jeremias, *TWNT*, IV, 860.

[86] Cf. e.g., R. Johanan's statement in *Ber.* 34b.

[87] The difficulty of detecting in all cases which sayings are directed toward the messianic era and which toward eternal life after the messianic era is notorious. For our purpose the distinction does not affect the argument and no judgment will thus be made in uncertain instances.

[88] *Song of Songs R.* VI.9.2, by the Tanna Judah b. Ilai; *Tanh.*, *pequdi* 3, 133a; jNed. III, 11; *Tem.* 16a; *Sanh.* 102a; *Mid. Teh.* Ps. 1, sec. 13.

for them. There too, the original light, hidden from the world because of its evil, will shine again.[89] The belief that the abode of the blessed was created by God before the world, or at least during the first week, surely shows the same interest in *gan 'eden* as a future paradise.[90]

In the light of the above the question must be asked whether any relationship exists between Adam and the eschaton. Here the answer is as clear as in the apocryphal and pseudepigraphal literature. The rabbis do not care about Adam as a concrete, actual individual. They do care about the reversal of the limitations upon human existence brought about by this person. Adam exists in rabbinic theology partly as a portrait of that nature promised to man. It is promised to man in the future because it was intended by God in the beginning.

The rabbis are, in fact, explicit. The most important logion here is that which lists six things lost to Adam to be restored in the world to come.[91] As we have already seen, three of these refer to Adam's nature itself. To be restored are his glory, his life, and his stature. In that day Gen. 3:22 will be read: 'Behold, the man has (now) become as one of us' (*Gen. R.* XXI.7). Confirmation of the parallelism can probably also be seen in the following logion. Some rabbis are concerned with the difference in spelling of the verb 'to form' (יצר) in Gen. 2:7 and 2:19. The first verse, which narrates the creation of man is spelled *plene*, וַיִּיצֶר; the second, which describes the creation of the animals, is spelled defectively, וַיִּצֶר. Of several explanations for this discrepancy, one is that the two *yods* in Gen. 2:7 hint at two formations of man, one for this life and the other for the life to come.[92] With the creation of the first man God has prepared the nature mankind will enjoy in the resurrection.[93] That some rabbinic sayings do

---

[89] For all these ideas cf. *Sifra, behuqotai* 3 (111*a*), on Lev. 26:12; *Mid. Teh.* Ps. 1, sec. 22; *Targ. Jon.* on Gen. 2:8; *Sanh.* 99*a*, 102*a*; *Song of Songs R.* VI.9.2; *Num. R.* XIII.2; *Tanh, šemini* 9 (16*b*). Some of these are Tannaitic in origin.

[90] *P.R.E.* 3; *Pes.* 54*a*; *Ned.* 39*b*; *Gen. R.* XV.3; *Targ. Jon.* on Gen. 2:8 and 3:24; *Targ. Jer.* on Gen. 3:24. See on this general motif also Strack-Billerbeck, *Kommentar zum Neuen Testament aus Talmud und Midrasch* (2d ed.; Munich, 1956), IV, 1148f.

[91] E.g., *Gen. R.* XII.6; cf. above p. 00.

[92] This notion is probably at least as old as the 1st century A.D. Cf. *Tanh., tazri'a* 1 (17*a*); *Mid. Teh.* Ps. 139, sec. 6; *Gen. R.* XIV.5.

[93] For another parallel between Adam and eschaton cf. *Gen. R.* XVIII.1.

not fit this correspondence is, of course, clear. It seems hard to deny, however, that the basic emphasis of the rabbis is upon the portrait of Adam as true man, the man who truly existed in that nature to be bestowed in the end of days.

The last three of the six things lost by Adam were deprivations of the cosmos rather than of human nature, and these also will be restored in the new age. The spontaneous bearing of plants and trees and the brilliance of the luminaries will all return at this time. Few sayings expand upon the bearing of plants and trees, probably because of the more spiritual existence usually thought of for the world to come.[94] On the other hand, much discussion is found about the return of the luminaries.[95] This event is usually thought to be the restoration of that original light created on the first day. God had hidden the light until the generation of the Messiah.[96] In addition to the above motifs, an echo still persists of the return of peace between animals and men in the new age.[97]

Adam as a concrete figure (that is, an actually existing man) is not mentioned at all in the sayings discussed above.[98] What returns is not Adam but Adam's nature. Nor is there much interest in return to a primeval and perfect cosmos. An anthropological concern underlies Adamic mythology, a concern which drives the theologians to depict what will be man's future on the basis of God's 'past', His perfect intent in creation.

Finally it should be emphasized that no evidence exists for the assertion of a relationship between Adam and Messiah, such that Adam is in any way involved in the process of Israel's redemption.

[94] Cf., however, *Sifra, behuqotai* sec. 1 (110b); *Gen. R.* X.4; *Exod. R.* XV.21.

[95] *Pesik. R.* XXXVI (161a–b); *Tanh., šemini* 9 (16b); implied in *Gen. R.* XVII.5; cf. also *Gen. R.* XII.6 and parallels. These materials are mostly Amoraic.

[96] E.g., *Pesik. R.* XXXVI (161a–b).

[97] *Gen. R.* XCV.1; *Exod. R.* XV.21.

[98] Two traditions, however, do seem to imply some interest in Adam's personal fate at the eschaton. *Gen. R.* XXI.7 contains the discussion as to whether or not Adam is to be allowed to return in the future world. R. Judah and R. Nehemiah argue this point, and it does seem that Adam rather then mankind is the subject. In *Gen. R.* XXI.1 a curious saying occurs in which Adam is highly venerated. He appears to be living in heaven and his space or partition (מחיצה) is closer to God's throne than is that of the angels. Furthermore the passage, which is a *pešer* on Dan. 8:13, accepts the word 'sanctuary' (*qodeš*) as referring to the first man. Yet the section alludes to Adam's sin and speaks of his being declared righteous at the eschaton. Although the date of the logion is impossible to decide, the text bases itself upon the translation of Aquilas, a Tanna. These passages are, however, surprising just because the ideas they contain are not echoed in the Adamic traditions at large.

Only a few traditions draw together the two figures.[99] Just these
logia show conclusively that (a) Adam is no actual figure in the
eschatological events and (b) the Messiah is largely a symbol for
God's act. What is said is not that the Messiah redeems but that
redemption comes *in the days of* the Messiah.[100] The contrast in
the logia is not between the two figures, but between the two aeons,
this world and the world to come, more specifically between
Adam's original and man's eschatological existence.

Two further places have indeed been argued as Adam/Messiah
speculation by Staerk and Murmelstein, but although on the
surface the arguments are plausible, they do not stand up under
critical investigation.[101] The first concerns the saying: 'The Son
of David will not come before all the souls in the *gup* [גוף] have
been exhausted.' The word *gup*, the literal meaning of which is
'body', is claimed by these scholars to be the body of Adam.
Since all souls are in some way pre-existent in Adam, they must
pass from Adam to Messiah before the ultimate salvation can
arrive. Now it is true that at least one text speaks of souls being in
Adam (*Exod. R.* XL.3), and other texts say that all souls must be
exhausted before Messiah can appear. But on what grounds are
these unrelated sayings joined together? Does *gup* really refer to
the body of Adam? In at least six places there occurs the notion
of a predetermined number of persons who must be born before
Messiah can come.[102] Of these six, four use the word *gup*.[103]
Gen. R. XXIV.4, however, says that 'King Messiah is not to
come until all the persons which God determined to create have
been formed'. The text of *Qoheleth Rabbah* I.6 is very similar.
Thus *gup* does not even have to belong to the saying. Furthermore

[99]Almost all of these have already been discussed. The return of Adam's
nature in the days of the Messiah, e.g., *Gen. R.* XII.6; *Exod. R.* XV.21; the
return of the luminary in the days of the Messiah, *Pesik. R.* XXXVI (161*a–b*).
Cf. also *Targ. Jon.* and *Targ. Jer.* on Gen. 3:15.

[100] Only in the probably late logion in *Pesik. R.* XXXVI (161*b*) does the
Messiah seem to play an active role in salvation. See on this also P. Volz, *Die
Eschatologie der jüdischen Gemeinde* (Tübingen, 1934), pp. 173ff.

[101] Staerk, *Soter II*, pp. 125ff.; Murmelstein, *WZKM*, XXXV (1928),
264; cf. above, p. xiii.

[102]*A.Z.* 5*a*; *Nid.* 13*b*; *Yeb.* 62*a* and 63*b*; *Eccles. R.* I.6; *Gen. R.* XXIV.4;
Meyer lists a seventh, *Tanh. B.*, *neṣabim* 8, but its relevance seems doubtful;
cf. R. Meyer, *Hellenistisches in der rabbinischen Anthropologie* (Stuttgart, 1937),
p. 61. The saying, while its origin is disputed by the rabbis, is probably
Tannaitic. *A.Z.* 5*a* claims it for R. Jose, a Tanna.

[103]*A.Z.* 5*a*; *Nid.* 13*b*; *Yeb.* 62*a* and 63*b*.

F

this word is never defined as Adam's body, and without such evidence, the judgment of Staerk and Murmelstein remains highly questionable. Particularly is this so because *gup* is more likely a place not in Adam but in the heavenly courts.[104]

An even clearer violation of careful exegesis is Murmelstein's argument that the staff of Adam is transmitted to King Messiah.[105] The saying has already been discussed which tells of Adam's staff and its eventual transmission to Moses (*P.R.E.*40). An entirely separate tradition (of which there is only one appearance, to my knowledge) narrates how Aaron's staff was used by the kings of Israel, then divinely hidden away, to be held one day by King Messiah (*Num. R.* XVIII.23). This logion even raises the question whether Aaron's rod once belonged to Moses; *some* rabbis say, it suggests, that this was so. There is no justification for relating the two traditions and to argue that they prove Adam's staff was transmitted to the Messiah. The conclusion seems inescapable: the rabbis are *not* interested in making Adam into a savior figure who has a personal involvement in the acts or results of the eschatological events.

[104] Volz translates the word as *Vorratskammer*, or storeroom; *Eschatologie*, p. 140. Meyer similarly believes the *gup* to be an antechamber in heaven; *Hellenistiches*, pp. 61f. He thinks the concept includes the idea of a real pre-existence of souls and shows the influence of Greek philosophy. However that may be, the prior history of the idea in Jewish theology probably goes back to a notion of chambers for the souls of the righteous dead. While waiting for the eschaton the souls inhabit these heavenly places; cf. IV Ez. 4:35; II Bar. 23:5; *Eccles. R.* III.21; *Gen. R.* XXI.1. Perhaps under the influence of Greek ideas Jewish theology next posited similar chambers for those souls yet unborn.

[105] Murmelstein, *WZKM*, XXXVI (1929), 55.

CHAPTER IV

PAUL: THE NEW AND THE OLD CREATION

Since Jewish theologians used the figure of Adam to exhibit their views about man, the question must be raised whether Paul is also basically involved in an anthropology when he speaks of the first and the Last Adam. Bultmannian exegesis interprets all of Paul's theology from an anthropological standpoint, and the popularity of this approach has predisposed scholars, perhaps too readily, to ask first about Paul's views of man and only secondly about his Christology.[1] Cogent objections to Bultmann's methodology are possible.[2] Nevertheless I hope to show in the following chapters that Paul's Christology of the Last Adam is primarily directed toward illuminating and assuring the Christian's hope of eschatological humanity. It should be stressed, however, that although the believer now already possesses in a provisional way his future life, it essentially remains a gift to be hoped for. To see the true man as a complete reality in the present, the believer can look only to Christ the Lord, who as Last Adam is the man God intends all men to be. Christology cannot be dissolved into anthropology; rather anthropology is derived from Christology.

The first step must be to discuss Paul's description of man, in order to provide the proper context for understanding the purpose of his Adamic Christology.[3] The Apostle, of course, speaks of the

---

[1] Cf. R. Bultmann, *New Testament Theology*, I, 190f.

[2] E. Käsemann, for example, argues with some justification against what he considers to be the too subjective and individualistic interpretation of Paul by Bultmann; cf. *ZTK*, LVIII (1961), 367–78. Bultmann has replied to this in ΔΙΚΑΙΟΣΥΝΗ ΘΕΟΥ, *JBL*, LXXXIII (1964), 12–16.

[3] The kind of anthropological analysis Bultmann has made popular—analysis of Paul's use of terms such as flesh, body, soul, mind, etc.—is certainly an important tool but is not particularly helpful here; cf. Bultmann, *Theology*, I, 191–249. When Paul is speaking about what man is or will be, he is thinking of man in his totality, even though he uses phrases like living according to the flesh, the renewal of the mind, or the redemption of the body. Bultmann has made all this quite clear. When Paul speaks of image or glory he is talking there too about man in his total existence, and there is little to be gained by relating the Bultmannian analysis to our discussion. The one major exception concerns the present existence of the new humanity, which will be discussed in chapter V.

old man as well as the new. It is impossible, however, to begin
first with a description of the man of sin and death. Not only is
Paul more interested in the new creation, but his views of the man
of this world also cannot really be understood except by contrast
with those of man in that world now coming into existence. Paul
puts the two natures in contrast, as Jewish theologians were accus-
tomed to do. But whereas his contemporaries tend to contrast the
past (the first Adam) with the present, Paul uses only a contrast of
the present with the future (the Last Adam).

To find the proper anthropological perspective from which to
view Paul's statements is not, however, as easy as it might appear.
Many scholars, particularly Bultmann and those influenced by
him, have rejected any substantival approach.[4] Paul thinks of the
whole man, not of parts such as body or soul, and understands
man to be what he does. Here the decisional, existential life of
man is seen as the real arena of humanity. The understanding of
man as substance or nature is said to be Hellenistic or gnostic
and, in fact, an understanding against which Paul fights. Even
where the Apostle uses what apparently are terms for substance,
what he really means by these terms, it is argued, is still non-
substantial. Paul changes space into time, the substantial into the
historical.

To argue against this view is difficult, for clearly it has brought
significant insight into the depths of the Apostle's thought. And
yet I believe that the attempt to exclude rigidly the substantival
side of Pauline anthropology is a movement away from a correct
interpretation. One implication of the previous chapters is that
early Jewish theologians had a substantival view of man, fallen and
eschatological, which they were able, however naively this might
seem to modern thinkers, to harmonize naturally and without
reflection with their strong ethical and decisional understanding.
The same thing is true for Paul, as I hope the following pages will
show.

I think it quite correct to say that Paul views man as a unity,

---

[4] For Bultmann cf., for an example, his discussion of σῶμα in *Theology*,
I, 192–203, although Bultmann is more careful than some other commentators.
Many other scholars could be mentioned here, but particularly clear statements
will be found in E. Fuchs, *Christus und der Geist bei Paulus* (Leipzig, 1932),
pp. 11–73; Käsemann, *Leib und Leib Christi*, pp. 97–135; Wilckens, *Weisheit
und Torheit*, pp. 214–24; Schweizer, *TWNT*, VI, 422–31.

the totality of man as an acting *being*. To make him have this totality in mind in every passage, however, is to expect too much. Paul looks at various aspects of man's existence according to the point he happens to be making. Thus he may wrestle with the ethical life of the Christian without ever giving a hint that he sees man to be anything besides decision and act. At other places he emphasizes the new eschatological nature without speaking ethically at all. This is entirely a natural and even inevitable process for an unsystematic thinker like the Apostle. An injustice is done to him when we recoil from some statement because he has not right then and there added the necessary qualifiers. For example: 'Paul is here a gnostic because he describes the new humanity without mentioning faith and the ethical life.' The next step is to separate what he says from what he means on the theory that what he says is gnostic or substantival, but what he *must* mean (since he is not a gnostic) is decisional.

All of this is unnecessary and indeed potentially misleading. Paul, like his Jewish contemporaries, thinks of man substantively as well as decisionally, and he does not intend to separate man's eschatological humanity from the ethical quality this humanity is to demonstrate. The new nature is not an ineradicable gift, independent of the believer's quality of life. But it *is* a gift, given prior to man's achievement and out of which his achievement comes. The *extra nos* of the Christ event is not simply the reconciliation of the cross; it is also the life of the resurrection through the Spirit. In fact Paul's emphasis upon the new nature as gift is one of the strongest affirmations in all the New Testament of the radical grace of God through Christ. The statements centering about the eschatological humanity of the Last Adam tend to speak of the new nature more than the new obedience. This means only that a constant reminder is needed that the new obedience is always to be assumed as an inseparable center of the new humanity whether or not Paul makes this explicit in each passage.

The New Creation

Basic to Paul's kerygma is the affirmation that Christ has brought to man, and therefore to the cosmos, the renewed existence Jews hoped for in the world to come: man is a new creation. Though the term 'new creation', καινὴ κτίσις, is found only

twice in the genuine Pauline literature,[5] the phrase certainly
expresses the basis upon which Paul builds his eschatological
anthropology. 'Therefore, if any one is in Christ, he is a new
creation; the old has passed away, behold the new has come.'[6]   In
Galatians 6:15 the phrase recurs: 'For neither circumcision
counts for anything, nor uncircumcision, but a new creation.'
The thought also underlies I Corinthians 7:31. Here Paul enjoins
the community to cease from living attached to the world. 'This
world' with all its values is rejected, 'For the form of this world is
passing away'. Paul assumes here the basic Jewish division into
two aeons, this age and the age to come. But since the world to
come is a new *creation*, it is apparent that Paul has accepted the
Urzeit-Endzeit formulation so characteristic of the Judaism of his
day.

Two things can well be said at this point. The first is that the
question whether the new creation is 'simply' a return to the
conditions of the original creation, or whether it indicates something superior, probably would not have occurred to Paul.
Nowhere in biblical or Jewish thought is it suggested that God's
intention at creation was inferior; indeed, such a view would have
foundered on the notion of God's mercy and grace. On the other
hand, neither Paul nor his contemporaries were forced to describe
this original perfection within the limitations of the Old Testament.
As should already be clear, Jewish theology often used more

---

[5] There is still no complete consensus as to what represents the genuine
corpus of the Epistles. Accepted in this study is the judgment of F. W. Beare
that 'the opinion now most prevalent among the few who are competent to
judge of such matters is that Philemon and Colossians are from the hand of
Paul, but that Ephesians is the work of a disciple of the second generation';
IB, XI, 133. Many scholars, however, reject Colossians. II Thessalonians
does not affect our discussion so a decision upon it here is irrelevant. Judgment
is uncertain, moreover, about two passages within the Epistles which relate to
our discussion. The majority of modern exegetes have accepted Lohmeyer's
argument that Phil. 2:5–11 is pre-Pauline; cf. Ernst Lohmeyer, *Kyrios Jesus:
Eine Untersuchung zu Phil. 2, 5–11* ('Sitzungsberichte der Heidelberger Akademie
der Wissenschaften,' Phil.-hist. Klasse, No. 18; Heidelberg, 1928). Many
believe that Col. 1:15–20 is also pre-Pauline, although Moule and Beare are
among recent exegetes who accept its authenticity; cf. Beare, *IB*, XI, 162,
and C. F. D. Moule, *The Epistles of Paul the Apostle to the Colossians and to
Philemon* ('Cambridge Greek Testament,' N.S.; Cambridge, 1957), pp. 60f.
Had Paul disagreed with these hymns, he would hardly have quoted them;
they can thus be used to determine his thought. Furthermore, it is doubtful
whether these passages, with respect to our subject, add anything strikingly
new to what Paul says more clearly elsewhere.

[6] II Cor. 5:17. κτίσις may here mean 'creature,' but the meaning of the
phrase *vis-à-vis* man would be the same.

'super-historical' concepts than those found in the Old Testament to describe the content of the original perfection. Nor was there any rigid attempt to equate every detail of the *Endzeit* with the *Urzeit*. Yet though the description of the age to come differed to some extent from that of the creation, this does not mean that Judaism or Paul believed the new creation to be better in essence than the original.[7]

The second thing to be emphasized is that Paul does not use the term 'new creation' as a metaphor. Man in Christ will be, indeed already is, a truly new creature. The literal reference of Paul's language here has often been noticed,[8] but it needs to be reiterated to avoid any suggestion that Paul is speaking simply of some emotional, intellectual, or decisional experience of the natural man.[9] Paul's language implies further that the reality of

[7] Cf. N. A. Dahl, 'Christ, Creation, and the Church,' in *The Background of the New Testament and its Eschatology*, eds. W. D. Davies and D. Daube (Cambridge, 1956), p. 429. This amounts to a 'typological' view of history, which is neither circular nor 'straightlined.' Each event is a unique event; yet at the same time one event can be similar to other events because the intent of the Lord of history never ceases to be the same.

[8] Cf. Albert Schweitzer, *The Mysticism of Paul the Apostle* (New York, 1955), esp. pp. 13–18; A. E. J. Rawlinson, *The New Testament Doctrine of the Christ* (London, 1926), p. 154.

[9] Some recent attempts, for example, tend to make a radical distinction between the 'substantive' language of gnosticism and the ethical or decisional language of the Old Testament and Judaism. While Paul may be influenced by gnosticism, at heart he commits himself, it is argued, to the Old Testament viewpoint. Thus Jervell relates so closely Paul's ideas of δόξα and εἰκών to justification or righteousness that they seem practically synonymous. Thus he can deny that δόξα is a light-substance given to the believer and assert that it is, rather, the situation of justification; cf. *Imago Dei*, pp. 182f., 256, 281. Similarly Schweizer in *TWNT*, VI, 423ff., affirms that at basis Paul's notion of the Spirit is not a substantive concept, but rather relational, normative, closely related to faith. 'The union of the faithful with the *kyrios* is not given in a pneumatic material, but in the knowledge given by the *pneuma* of the one crucified for him' (p. 423). All such attempts may be good and necessary demythologization, but they are not thereby good exegesis. They overlook, for one thing, that Judaism thought substantively of δόξα and πνεῦμα, as earlier chapters indicate. That Paul thinks in relational terms when he speaks of justification and faith is obviously true. That he speaks always with this intent with other concepts is not obvious. It is even the case that the substantive new creation depends for its reality upon the relationship given in justification, but that the former term can be transformed into the latter is not true. No doubt Paul wants to emphasize that the new life is not an indelible possession of man but rather a gift which depends upon God's act in the cross and man's response of faith. But this does not mean that the new life is not 'something' to be possessed as long as man remains in faith. By returning to his former ways, man may lose the life he had begun to possess; cf. Gal. 3:3. Thus to hold that Paul thinks in a substantive manner about the new creation by no means entails the view that he has become a gnostic.

this new nature is nothing more nor less than a restoration to that truly human reality God has always desired for man. Most of Paul's categories are similar to those of his Jewish contemporaries.

1. The Apostle knows that eternal life awaits the believer in the new creation. Implied of course everywhere in Paul's writings, the hope comes to clearest expression in I Corinthians 15. Here he joyfully proclaims the resurrection and the gift of everlasting life. Whatever is the correct interpretation of 1 Corinthians 15:23ff.,[10] Paul clearly accepts the basic eschatological scheme, in which 'the last enemy to be destroyed is death'.[11] Occasionally Paul slips into usage similar to that of the rabbis and speaks of the future existence simply as 'life'. As already indicated, for the rabbis Adam will receive back his 'life' in the world to come. For Paul the life of Jesus is to be manifested in the bodies of the redeemed (II Cor. 4:18). He hopes that in the future 'what is mortal may be swallowed up by life'.[12]

2. Perhaps the most common characteristic applied to the new man, however, is that of 'glory', δόξα. The body of the resurrection is raised in glory (I Cor. 15:43). The man in Christ is being changed from glory into glory (II Cor. 3:18). An 'eternal weight of glory', αἰώνιον βάρος δόξης, awaits man in the new age (II Cor. 4:17). The redeemed will appear with Christ in glory (Col. 3:4). God has prepared the redeemed for glory.[13] Paul here repeats Jewish conceptions. Glory belongs first and foremost to God. God manifests His divine nature and power through this glory. Yet it was intended by God for man in creation and will be restored to him in the world to come.[14] Paul himself shows clearly in Rom. 5:2 that man's glory is derivative; here the glory man hopes for is God's glory. It belongs essentially also to Christ, and what awaits man is precisely this very glory which Christ possesses. Christians are 'heirs of God and fellow heirs with Christ, provided we suffer with him in order that we may also be glorified with him' (Rom. 8:17). At this point it becomes clear that Paul's hope for the renewal of man rests upon the power and being of Christ.

[10] The discussion revolves around the word τέλος in verse 24. Cf., e.g., Hans Lietzmann, *An die Korinther I.II* (4th ed.; 'H.N.T.'; Tübingen, 1949), p. 23; Davies, *Paul and Rabbinic Judaism*, pp. 293–95.

[11] I Cor. 15:26; cf. also Rom. 2:7, 5:21, Gal. 6:8, and elsewhere.

[12] II Cor. 5:4; cf. also Rom. 5:17.

[13] Rom. 9:23; also 2:10.

[14] Cf. above, pp. 26f., 48f., 55.

While it is no doubt true that this gift of δόξα is dependent upon, or is the completion of, justification,[15] δόξα is nevertheless a term Paul employs to speak of the eschatological *existence* to be bestowed upon man. One day man will radiate that very nature of glory which now shines in the countenance of Christ. The *RSV* translation of Phil. 3:21, 'Will change our lowly body to be like his glorious body', renders perhaps too weakly the Greek, σύμμορφον τῷ σώματι τῆς δόξης αὐτοῦ. Σύμμορφον here does not indicate a general, unessential likeness, but two forms which have the same 'visible' existence.[16] Despite Rom. 8:30 this glory will not be manifest until the consummation.

3. The eschatological man is also to possess a spiritual body. Though the language may be Paul's own, the concept itself is not novel to Judaism. Apparently in opposition to the traditional view of a completely corporeal resurrection, some Jewish theologians at least modified if not completely altered the old view. They held instead that the resurrection body would be a non-corporeal, or at least a non-fleshly body. This new existence of glory was more like that of angels and of stars than like the body of sin and death.[17]

Paul, perhaps influenced also by his Hellenistic environment, casts his lot with this position. 'I tell you this, brethren: flesh and blood cannot inherit the kingdom of God, nor does the perishable inherit the imperishable' (I Cor. 15:50). Again the resurrection chapter of I Corinthians speaks most tellingly.

So it is with the resurrection of the dead.
What is sown is perishable,
    What is raised is imperishable [ἀφθαρσία].
It is sown in dishonor,
    it is raised in glory [δόξης].
It is sown in weakness,
    it is raised in power [δυνάμει].

[15] Cf. Helmuth Kittel, *Die Herrlichkeit Gottes* (Giessen, 1934), p. 195.
[16] Cf. J. Behm, *TWNT*, IV, 753–60.
[17] Cf. II Bar. 51, I En. 104, Wisdom 3:1–4, Mk. 12:24f., and the discussion in Davies, *Paul and Rabbinic Judaism*, pp. 301–308. *Ber.* 17a, although very similar in tone to Mk. 12:24f., is too late to be of any value here. The notions ascribing to eschatological man a great, transcendent glory and angelic nature certainly move in the direction of a non-corporeal body, although no Jewish tradition, to my knowledge, links the Spirit with the new nature in the way that Paul does.

It is sown a physical body,
it is raised a spiritual body [σῶμα πνευματικόν].

. . . .

For the trumpet will sound, and the dead will be raised
imperishable, and we shall be changed [ἀλλαγησόμεθα].
For this perishable nature must put on the imperishable,
and this mortal nature must put on immortality.[18]

Here Paul wrestles with several terms, apparently acknowledging
the difficulty of speaking precisely about what cannot be known.
He seems to emphasize, by its climactic position, the term σῶμα
πνευματικόν, the 'spiritual body'. By this Paul at least means a
body foreign to any possibility within this world. The πνεῦμα
comes from outside, from God, and is itself an eschatological gift.
Moreover, the spiritual body is a direct gift from Christ who is
the life-giving Spirit, πνεῦμα ζωοποιοῦν (I Cor. 15:45). Thus the
spiritual body denotes a non-corporeal existence with its source in
the power of God's gift. Paul, everyone might well agree, did
wisely in not attempting a more precise description of eschatological man.[19]

The Spirit also brings the possibility of the perfection of man's
wisdom and ethical deeds. When Paul writes of the future consummation, he assumes these perfections; since, however, the
believer already possesses the first fruits of the Spirit, it becomes
a concern to the Apostle to show how in this life the Spirit works,
or ought to work, toward the completion of man. In contrast to
the weakness or ineffectiveness of man apart from grace, the
believer is given powers which Paul calls gifts of the Spirit.[20] The
catalogue is familiar: wisdom, healing, miracles, speaking in
tongues, prophecy, and, of course, love. Love as a spiritual gift
sums up the ethical ability of the believer, and elsewhere Paul calls
the life of love the fruit of the Spirit, or walking by the Spirit (Gal.

---

[18] I Cor. 15:42–44, 52b–53.

[19] Most exegetes also wisely refrain from suggesting too precise a meaning
for Paul. Moffatt, for example, suggests that the phrase 'spiritual body' is a
'semi-metaphysical' term, and explains *his* term to mean that 'the spiritual,
in other words, is not the immaterial'; cf. James Moffatt, *The First Epistle of
Paul to the Corinthians* ('M.N.T.C.'; New York, n.d.), pp. 259f. Weiss denies
that Paul is thinking of the Stoic soul substance but on the positive side can
only suggest that Paul uses the phrase almost as a '*Formbegriff*'; cf. Johannes
Weiss, *Der erste Korintherbrief* (9th ed.; 'K.E.K.'; Göttingen, 1910), pp. 372f.

[20] Cf. I Cor. 12–14; Rom. 12.

5:16–26). Thus the Spirit is the source of the radical change which is already beginning to take place, and this change leaves no part of man untouched. Jervell is so far correct in emphasizing that σῶμα ψυχικόν and σῶμα πνευματικόν in I Cor. 15 point not simply to matter or substance but to man in his totality.[21] Whether Paul is explicitly thinking of ethical powers in this passage is, however, another matter.

While the new man is to be spiritual in nature, he nevertheless is to possess a body, σῶμα. This emphasis distinguishes Paul's thought from the Greek concept of immortality of the soul and preserves for him the unity of man, as Judaism understood it. In one passage Paul links closely the adoption as sons in the age to come with the redemption of the body. 'We ourselves, who have the first fruits of the Spirit, groan inwardly as we wait for adoption as sons, the redemption of our bodies', τὴν ἀπολύτρωσιν τοῦ σώματος (Rom. 8:23). Such an identity exists between the man 'here' and the man 'there' that despite Paul's emphasis upon the difference of existence in the two ages he can speak of the gift in the future simply as the redemption of the σῶμα from the corruption to which it has been subject.

Paul may allude to the notion of a non-corporeal future existence in one other passage. In 1 Cor. 6:3 the Apostle admonishes the church not to go to civil courts to settle disputes which have arisen within the community. The church at Corinth does not seem to realize that it should have the insight to decide its own cases. Do they not know, Paul asks, that they are one day to judge the angels? The precise meaning here is uncertain.[22]

---

[21] *Imago Dei*, pp. 263ff. Bultmann argues that σῶμα means for Paul not the 'body' but man in his totality, especially as one who makes himself the object of his own action. Bultmann is aware that it is very hard to reconcile this definition with the use of the word in I Cor. 15, but he tries by making a distinction between the mythology of the resurrection which Paul has taken over and the Apostle's 'real intention'; cf. *Theology*, I, 192–99. Bultmann's treatment of σῶμα is in general highly enlightening, but Paul must not be held to a rigid consistency in a word as general as this. With respect to I Cor. 15, I believe the mythology is Paul's real intention.

[22] The judgment concerns all the angels, according to Robertson and Plummer, *First Epistle of St. Paul to the Corinthians* ('I.C.C.'; New York, 1911), p. 112; C. T. Craig, *IB*, X, 70; and E. B. Allo, *Première Épître aux Corinthiens* (2d ed.; Paris, 1956), p. 134; it concerns the evil angels, according to Moffatt, p. 64, Lietzmann, p. 25, and Weiss, p. 147; it has reference to intermediate powers, according to Jean Héring, *La Première Épître de Saint Paul aux Corinthiens* (Paris, 1949), p. 44. Weiss, pp. 147f., thinks that κρίνω refers to the act of judgment, while Robertson and Plummer, p. 112, and Moffatt, p. 64, believe it extends to general rulership.

Probably, however, the judging includes the idea of rulership. In the resurrection the saints are to rule over the angels. In view of the superiority which man (Adam) has over the angels in Jewish theology, the beings involved here need not be simply the wicked, rebellious group under Satan. Redeemed man is to be superior to all angels and is thus to exercise authority over them. Since angelic nature is non-corporeal, spiritual, Paul must imply by his statement an acceptance of the Jewish view that the nature of eschatological man is to be equal or superior to the nature of the angels.[23]

In all the above Paul asserts nothing which puts him in opposition to his Jewish background. Indeed, a perfect summary, formally at least, of the views of the Apostle can be found in the rabbinic dictum often cited in this study: Adam lost his glory, his life, and his stature because of the fall and will regain them when Messiah comes (*Gen. R.* XII.6). Paul agrees precisely with this saying in respect to glory and life. While he argues for a spiritual rather than a physical body in the eschaton, contrary to this particular rabbinic logion, he nevertheless is dealing with the same problem.

4. The Apostle is not, however, content with the usual Jewish set of concepts. He insists on injecting still a fourth term to describe what eschatological nature will be like, and this term, although appearing in the Old Testament, does not figure prominently in rabbinic discussions about Adam, except when Gen. 1:26f. is quoted.[24] Man in the new creation will be the image of God. Usually Paul chooses his language carefully to indicate just in what sense man is the image. Christ is the image of God.[25] The

[23] Cf. above, pp. 27f., 47f.

[24] In *B.B.* 58a occurs the story about R. Bana'ah, who was not allowed to survey Adam's tomb because Adam is God's likeness (יונק). Cf. also the parable in *Gen. R.* VIII.10 where the angels mistake Adam for God; here the motif of the image appears to be assumed. Neither of these refers to eschatological nature. The only passages I know which might relate the image to the new creation occur in *Gen. R.* XXI, where Gen. 3:22 is interpreted eschatologically as 'The man has now become as one of us.' Usually this verse is taken to refer to man's similarity with the angels, but once, in XXI.5, the similarity is said to be with God's nature. Cf. Jervell, *Imago Dei*, pp. 71–121. The actual use of the word outside of quotations of Gen. 1:26f. is not, however, as common as the vast amount of material Jervell has collected might suggest. According to Jervell, in so far as the concept of the image is related to *Heilsgeschichte*, it refers to the possibility of the Israelite's receiving this image at or after Sinai; cf. pp. 114–19. He does not suggest that the term was used in eschatological contexts.

[25] II Cor. 4:4; Col. 1:15.

believer becomes God's image only through Christ. He is transformed into that image in which Christ now exists. Here is a strict identity between Christ and the believer. Man is not simply modeled after the image of Christ, nor does a hierarchy exist in which Christ is the middle term between God and man.[26]

In Rom. 8:29 Paul suggests that the Christian is destined to be conformed to the image of the Son of God. 'For those whom he foreknew he also predestined to be conformed to the image of his Son, in order that he might be the first-born among many brethren, συμμόρφους τῆς εἰκόνος τοῦ υἱοῦ αὐτοῦ. Here the image does not refer to a stamp or reflection which comes from the Son, but rather to that stamp which the Son himself is. The συμ- in συμμόρφους does not weaken the identity of believer and Christ; rather Paul stresses in this way the necessary connection between the two. In I Cor. 15:49 Paul does say that the new man is to bear the image of the heavenly man, but the parallelism of the verse indicates that identity rather than an imperfect copy is the relation asserted. 'Just as we have borne the image of the man of dust, we shall also bear the image of the man of heaven.' Man has lived his old life in the form of corporeal humanity; he will live his new life in the form of a spiritual humanity. II Cor. 3:18 echoes the above passages. The believer who is beholding the glory of God (that is, Christ) is being 'transformed into the same image', τὴν αὐτὴν εἰκόνα μεταμορφούμεθα, from one degree of glory into the next. The phrase, τὴν αὐτὴν εἰκόνα, means that the new nature is to be identical with the image of God, that is, Christ.

Col. 3:10 also points in the same direction. Here Paul speaks of the new man being renewed in knowledge according to the image of his Creator, τὸν νέον [ἄνθρωπον] τὸν ἀνακαινούμενον εἰς ἐπίγνωσιν κατ' εἰκόνα τοῦ κτίσαντος αὐτόν. Allusion to Gen. 1 is unmistakable. With most recent commentators, τοῦ κτίσαντος is best taken in conjunction with κατ' εἰκόνα as a reference to God. The object of the participle, αὐτόν, refers not to Christ but to the

---

[26] Jervell insists that Christ is εἰκὼν τοῦ θεοῦ, while the Christian is modeled κατ' εἰκόνα. Christ is *Vorbild;* the believer, *Abbild;* cf. *Imago Dei*, pp. 276ff. Only in Col. 3:10, however, is the new man κατ' εἰκόνα, and the context indicates that while Christ may be in Paul's mind as the Image, the believer is really κατ' εἰκόνα with reference to God, so that Christ and believer are each the image of God. Cf. below for the argument.

redeemed man of the new creation.[27] While nothing in the sentence forces one to take κατ' εἰκόνα as a reference to Christ,[28] Masson is perhaps correct, especially when the Colossians' passage is understood in conjunction with the ones discussed above, in believing that Christ is the image of God in the passage. According to this scholar, the image of God is the goal of man's renewal, and Christ as the Last Adam is the image to which man will conform.[29] Even so, however, man does not become an image of Christ, but the image of God, conformable to Christ who now already exists as that image. For Paul, then, man will one day be restored to the image of God. The Apostle uses the concept essentially as an eschatological term and looks ahead, rather than to primeval time, for its realization.[30] Christ plays the essential role, as we shall see in detail later, of being the mediator of this eschatological humanity; it is for this reason that Paul speaks of man as image of God only in terms of Christ.

⌐ Paul is here in clear contrast with the rabbis, for the latter avoided using the word 'image' in eschatological descriptions. According to Jervell, the rabbis thought that the image lost by Adam was regained, at least as a possibility, at Sinai, with the giving of the Torah.[31] In the few logia about Sinai in which the word occurs, however, 'image' is a substantive, not an ethical concept. It is truer to say that for the rabbis the renewal of the image *depends upon* obedience to the Torah. If this is so, it points to one way in which Paul, in opposition to Judaism, has put the Spirit in the place of the Torah. The possibility of an ethical

---

[27] Cf. Moule, *Colossians and Philemon*, p. 284; J. B. Lightfoot, *St. Paul's Epistle to the Colossians* (2d ed.; London, 1876), pp. 215f.; E. F. Scott, *The Epistles of Paul to the Colossians, to Philemon, and to the Ephesians* ('M.N.T.C.'; New York, 1930), p. 69; Charles Masson, *L'Épître de Saint Paul aux Colossiens* ('C.N.T.'; Neuchatel, 1950), p. 144.

[28] Scott, *Colossians*, p. 69, argues that Paul does not have Christ in mind here.

[29] *Colossiens*, p. 144. It should be noted, however, that Masson believes this passage, 3:5–11, to be probably deutero-Pauline; cf. pp. 144f.

[30] So C. K. Barrett, *Epistle to the Romans*, p. 170. It is to be noted that in I Cor. 11:7 Paul refers to man in his present existence as image and glory of God, with obvious allusion to the creation narratives in Gen. 1f. This must be seen as an exception to Paul's usual practice, for which δόξα is an eschatological term. Man does not possess this δόξα any more than he retains the image; cf. Rom. 3:23. Paul has 'lapsed' here into non-eschatological thinking. He does consider the new age to be somehow present within the believer now, but to take the Corinthians passage in this sense is to ignore the most natural interpretation of the text.

[31] *Imago Dei*, pp. 91f. Cf. above, p. 53f.

existence is given not by the law but by the Spirit.[32] This explains why Paul must use image as an eschatological term. Since it is the Spirit that works righteousness, only in the new creation can the image be regained that Adam once possessed. Again it cannot be maintained that Paul in using εἰκών is thinking explicitly of ethical existence; nothing in the contexts would justify such a suggestion. What can be argued, however, is that Paul's understanding of εἰκών includes the ethical as part of man's total life in the new creation.

Related to his affirmation of man's new nature is Paul's judgment that the cosmos will also be redeemed from its present state of corruption. We have already seen that Jewish theologians maintained this hope in their eschatology.[33] In contrast to some rabbinic statements which depict the new world in the most material terms, however, Paul speaks only in an allusive and a most cautious manner. In I Cor. 7:31 the Apostle says that the form, σχῆμα, of this world is passing away. Presumably the present world is to give way to a new world or a new σχῆμα of the world. If σχῆμα retains its meaning as a role played by an actor, the analogy may suggest that the present world has finished its role and is to be superseded by another.[34] The sparseness of this casual mention by Paul is alleviated only slightly by Rom. 8:18–23. Here Paul contrasts present and future for the cosmos in much the same way as he does for the individual in I Cor. 15.[35] Again, however, what emerges is primarily an affirmation of the extreme change that is to take place, rather than a precise description. 'For the creation itself will be liberated from the bondage of corruption to the freedom of that glory which the children of God possess' (translation mine). τῆς δόξης is best taken not as a qualifying phrase to ἐλευθερίαν, as the *RSV* suggests, but rather as the ruling term in the last phrase. Barrett is correct, I think, in

---

[32] It should be noted, however, that the Qumran community at times also based the new ethical existence upon the Holy Spirit; cf. 1QS 4:21 and 1QH 16: 12. The author(s) of the Psalms know(s) that the Holy Spirit rests upon him (1QH 7:6f., 9:32), although the Spirit in the Psalms is primarily the source of knowledge and wisdom. Cf. Nötscher, 'Geist und Geister in den Texten von Qumran,' *Mélanges Bibliques en l'honneur de André Robert* (Paris, 1957), pp.306–309, and W. Foerster, 'Der heilige Geist im Spätjudentum,' *NTS*, VIII (1961/ 62), 122–34.

[33] Cf. above, p. 56.   [34] So Héring, *Corinthiens*, p. 58.

[35] It is doubtful that Brunner is correct in seeing the historical rather than the physical order as the subject of this section; cf. Emil Brunner, *The Letter to the Romans* (London, 1959), pp. 74f.

suggesting that 'the glory of the children of God' is a single concept and is to be read in parallelism with 'corruption'.[36] Paul argues that the cosmos is destined for an existence of 'glory' similar to but not necessarily identical with that glory to be enjoyed by eschatological man.[37] At the eschaton God will change the world to an existence of pure light or glory.[38] Just what this might mean, that is, just what sort of world this would be, and what its relation to man, Paul does not care to speculate about.[39]

What may be of importance to note is that the release of the cosmos from corruption depends upon the event of man's salvation.[40] In this passage of Romans Paul is clearly reflecting upon the Genesis narrative. Just as the subjection of the cosmos was due to man's sin (though by God's decree), so the release will be due to man's redemption from sin. In effect this means that the cosmos as well as man looks to the Last Adam for salvation.

The Old Creation

Taken with the events of Christ and the church, Paul is directly concerned with the new creation which God is bringing to man and cosmos. He is only secondarily interested in the old creation which is passing away. Here lies, for example, a significant difference in tone between Paul and the author of IV Ezra. Both see this world as under the burden of sin and corruption; but while IV Ezra feels himself entirely a part of the old creation and yearns wistfully for release, Paul rejoices that the new has already come, at least in part. This world stands condemned precisely because it has not accepted the gift of the new creation. Thus Paul prefers exploring the ramifications of the new order to excoriating the old. Yet he does express his evaluation and judgment upon the man of sin—and this in the clearest of terms. Since this side of Paul's theology is well-known, it is only necessary here to relate his judgments upon the old creation to his hopes for the new.

[36] *Romans*, p. 166.
[37] There are different degrees of glory; cf. I Cor. 15:40f.
[38] So Dodd, *The Epistle to the Romans* ('M.N.T.C.'; London, 1932), p. 134.
[39] One does wonder whether Paul relates eschatological existence to the paradise in *gan'eḏen*. In II Cor. 12:2f. Paul seems to imply a vision of the paradise in the third heaven. Does he think this is to be the abode of the righteous in the new age?
[40] Cf. Paul Althaus, *Der Brief an die Römer* (6th ed.; 'N.T.D.'; Göttingen, 1949), p. 78: 'Die Geschichte der Menschheit mit Gott ist das schlagende Herz der ganzen Welt.'

1. *Man now lacks eternal life*. Paul clearly interprets the fall as that event which introduced death into the world. According to Rom. 5:12 death has entered into and spread abroad over all the world. Man is in bondage to corruption, φθορά, according to I Cor. 15:50. Here Paul repeats the Jewish view that death is not a natural phenomenon but is the judgment of God upon sin. Some commentators have seen in Paul contradictory views about the cause of death.[41] In Romans 5 Paul, it is argued, sees death as a penalty due to the sin of Adam; in I Corinthians 15 death appears rather as a natural phenomenon within the world. This contradiction is surely only apparent. Judaism was single-minded in its belief that death was associated with Adam and/or sin. Thus to discount Romans 5 as Paul's basic affirmation is difficult indeed. The main problem in I Corinthians 15 is that Paul uses an analogy taken from nature, which might seem to imply that the process from death to eternal life is a natural growth. Just as the seed must be buried before it can rise to life, so death is part of the order of the cosmos. Such an implication, however, takes the analogy too far and too literally. The Apostle's basic point is the difference between the physical body and the spiritual, and the analogy may intend to say no more than that. Furthermore, Paul does not necessarily see present nature as 'natural'. The cosmos is also under the bondage of corruption (Rom. 8:18ff.).

2. *Man now lacks the glory of God*. In Rom. 3:23 Paul suggests that the loss of glory is caused by sin. 'All have sinned and (thus) lack the glory of God.'[42] Though he does not explicitly relate this loss to Adam's disobedience, such a thought cannot be far from his mind.[43] As a result of sin man no longer possesses that glory which he had in the beginning. In Phil. 3:21 the body

[41] Cf. Bultmann, *Theology*, I, 249, and the discussion in A. M. Dubarle, *Le Péché originel dans l'Écriture* (Paris, 1958), pp. 151–56.

[42] Trans. mine. The usual English translation of ὑστερέω, 'to fall short of,' tends to be misleading. It is not a question of man exhausted in his efforts to attain the goal, which is δόξα θεοῦ, but rather of his lack of the gift he originally possessed. Ernst Kühl, *Der Brief des Paulus an die Römer* (Leipzig, 1913), p. 109, says ὑστερέω signifies the temporal and spatial separation of one thing from another. Lietzmann, *An die Römer* (4th ed.; 'H.N.T.'; Tübingen, 1933), p. 49, and Barrett, *Romans*, p. 74, relate the verse to the sin of Adam. Barrett interpets the verse to mean that 'man now lacks what he might now have had, that is, the glory with which Adam was created and which he (and all mankind with him) lost through sin.' Bultmann also believes the verse intends a relation with Adam; cf. his 'Ursprung und Sinn der Typologie als hermeneutischer Methode,' in *Pro Regno Pro Sanctuario*, pp. 92f.

[43] Cf. below, p. 75, note 3, for a discussion of Rom. 1:23.

G

of glory is contrasted with the present body of lowliness, τὸ σῶμα τῆς ταπεινώσεως. In I Cor. 15:43 the contrasting term is ἀτιμία, 'dishonor', although in this series of contrasts it is not entirely clear whether Paul is thinking of the body of the man while alive or of the body when dead. Judaism related the loss of glory to a loss of the powers which a man possessed.[44] In I Cor. 15:43b one finds a similar idea. Present weakness, ἀσθενεία, will be replaced by power, δύναμις. 'It is sown in weakness, it is raised in power.' The body bereft of glory is bereft of strength; it is weak, useless, futile, feeble. In Rom. 5:6 Paul again uses ἀσθενής to describe man's plight before redemption, and the *RSV* strikingly translates the verse, 'While we were yet helpless, at the right time Christ died for the ungodly.' Here ἀσθενής may contain ethical overtones. When speaking of δόξα, however, Paul is thinking of man's total exaltation, so that perhaps in the passage in Romans he has in mind man's total weakness. The σῶμα of flesh and blood, of corruption, is not able (οὐ δύναται) to inherit the Kingdom of God. Christ bestows through the gift of the Spirit a new religious and ethical possibility *and* a new nature.

3. *Man has become a sinner.* When Paul speaks of the 'old man', he devotes most of his time to a description of the situation of sin or hostility toward God. All men have sinned and have suffered condemnation.[45] This has meant a disruption of peace (Col. 1:20), caused by man's essential hostility toward God.[46] Sin is also disobedience to God's demand (Rom. 5:19). It is living by the flesh rather than by the Spirit.[47] Paul amplifies these judgments in many places, but there is no need here to pursue them any further.

What has been shown gives sufficient indication that the old and the new creations are mutually exclusive (although the believer still partakes of both) and that Paul understands the old in terms of its complete lack of the gifts bestowed in the new. Now it is possible to search for the sources of these two existences. We find them in his theology of the first and the Last Adam.

---

[44] Cf. above, p. 35, n. 13. The rabbis claimed that Adam had lost his original powers because of the fall.
[45] Rom. 3:23; 5:16.
[46] Rom. 5:10; 8:7; Col. 1:21; cf. also II Cor. 5:18f.
[47] E.g. Gal. 5:16–6:10.

CHAPTER V

PAUL: THE FIRST AND THE LAST ADAM

In all of Paul's writings no serious competitor to Adam as the originator of man's bondage to sin and death can be found. In places, especially Rom. 7, the Apostle speaks of sin as if it were an independent, controlling power in the world. Bultmann, however, seems correct in labeling this language as figurative and rhetorical.[1] His judgment is more questionable when he suggests that in Romans Paul is inconsistent with himself.[2] In the early chapters (1:18–3:20) Paul appears to argue for the guilt character of sin; all men stand under God's judgment. Here no mention is made of Adam, nor did the Apostle have him in mind.[3] If he had, Bultmann concludes, Paul could not have emphasized the guilt of all men, since Adam as cause of sin effectually eliminates such guilt. In view of Rom. 5 and I Cor. 15, however, Adam must be everywhere assumed as the originator of sin; but this does not mean, as is argued below, that individual guilt is taken away in Rom. 5.

[1] *New Testament Theology*, I, 245.
[2] Ibid., pp. 250f.
[3] Two attempts have recently been made to suggest that Adam does figure in the early chapters of Romans, especially 1:23; cf. Jervell, *Imago Dei*, pp. 312–31, and M. D. Hooker, 'Adam in Romans I,' *NTS*, VI (1959/60), 297–306. While each attempt differs in its treatment of the text in relation to Adam, both begin with the same observation: the language of Rom. 1:18ff. borrows from the LXX of Gen. 1. Miss Hooker argues that this section in Romans describes the path of sin which Adam took. God manifested his truth to Adam; Adam refused to listen and his heart became darkened. He gave allegiance to the serpent and thus became an idolater. Rabbinic tradition about Eve's sin as sexual in character explains Paul's mention of sexual perversion as a result of the sin. Miss Hooker also mentions the contrast between the glory of God and corruptible men in 1:23 as indicating the rabbinic view of the loss of glory by Adam. Jervell makes this last point his chief argument. Rom. 1:23 speaks not about idolatry but about the loss of δόξα by Adam: φάσκοντες εἶναι σοφοὶ ἐμωράνθη αν, καὶ ἤλλαξαν τὴν δόξαν τοῦ ἀφθάρτου θεοῦ ἐν ὁμοιώματι εἰκόνος φθαρτοῦ ἀνθρώπου καὶ πετεινῶν καὶ τετραπόδων καὶ ἑρπετῶν. The 'corruptible man' refers explicitly to Adam. Man becomes the image of Adam; cf. I Cor. 15:49. The mention of animals in 1:23 alludes to the rabbinic notion that by his sin Adam became like the animals.

That Paul in this section has in mind all men and not simply the Gentiles

Also there is the fact that Paul refers to the deception of Eve
by the serpent in II Cor. 11:2f. 'I feel a divine jealousy for you,
for I betrothed you to Christ to present you as a pure bride to her
one husband. But I am afraid that as the serpent deceived Eve
by his cunning, your thoughts will be led astray from a sincere and
pure devotion to Christ.' As many commentators suggest, the
imagery probably depends on the rabbinic idea that the serpent
actually had intercourse with Eve.[4] Yet the metaphor is not used
to discuss the origin of sin but rather the seduction of minds from
loyalty to Christ. Quite clearly Paul knew the rabbinic *haggadah*
about Eve, but he does not use it for the purpose of making her the
originator of sin as did some rabbis.

The centrality of Adam in the history of sin and death is
clearly stated in the two famous passages, Rom. 5-12–21 and I
Cor. 15:21f., 45–49. Since these passages will be constantly
before us for the remainder of the study, it may prove clearer to
discuss at this time a few of the crucial points of exegesis which
affect our treatment of both Adam and Christ.

Romans 5:12–21

Rom. 5–8 is a self-contained section with several formal
characteristics different from the sections that precede and follow.
One of these is that it is composed of several small semi-inde-
pendent units much like a homiletic midrash. The major theme
of the whole section is life in Christ. This theme is underscored

---

is an attractive argument. Furthermore, Gen. 1. does seem to be reflected in
Paul's language. This in itself does not prove the Adamic reference, however,
since the Apostle might well be thinking of creation entirely apart from Adam.
Paul does refer to the animals mentioned in Gen. 1, but surely because he finds
listed there the creatures which sinful man has come to worship instead of their
creator. I find the arguments for allusion to Adam at basis weak. Hooker's
suggestions are possible but not probable. Jervell's argument that man has
exchanged the glory of God for the image of Adam would be sound except for
the words that follow, καὶ πετεινῶν καὶ τετραπόδων καὶ ἑρπετῶν. That these words
refer to Adam's mortal nature rather than to idolatry cannot be substantiated
in view of the context. Thus the δόξα of verse 23 must refer to the glory which
shines from God rather than that which rests, or rested, upon Adam. Obscurities
in the verse do exist, but that they are solved by seeing here a reference to
Adam is dubious.

[4] Cf. Lietzmann, *An die Korinther I.II*, p. 145; R. H. Strachan, *The Second
Epistle of Paul to the Corinthians* ('M.N.T.C.'; New York, n.d.), p. 18; Hans
Windisch, *Der zweite Korintherbrief* (9th ed.; 'K.E.K.'; Göttingen, 1925),
p. 323. Cf. *Yeb.* 103*b*.

at the end of each sub-section by either an explicit or implicit affirmation of the eternal life which awaits the believer.[5] Every sub-section deals with some facet of the major theme, but there is no need to expect always a logical or sequential order among the units. Among other things this means that the continual attempt by commentators to find an explicit antecedent for the introductory phrase to 5:12–21, διὰ τοῦτο, 'therefore', will always be frustrated. Here it is used as an indefinite particle, loosely tying one sub-section to another. This of course does not imply that the sub-sections have no relation with each other. Not only is the broad theme of life in Christ present in all of them, but also, as is so characteristic of Paul's style, key words and minor motifs are here introduced and later picked up again and developed. The introductory unit, 5:1–11, thus sets the stage for much that is to follow. It announces the presence of justification on the one hand (pointing backwards to the conclusion of the previous section) and the hope for eschatological glory on the other (5:1, 2). The basis of our justification is God's love in the cross of Christ, and the basis of our hope is God's love in the Holy Spirit. What evokes Paul's amazement is that Christ dies not for the righteous or even for the good but for all of unrighteous mankind (5:6–8). The Apostle returns to this idea in 5:12–21, which explains in different terms how it is that mankind was ungodly and what the cross means for this humanity.[6] Yet the main goal of both sections remains that of affirming the hope for the glory of God and everlasting life.

The first verse of the section 5:12–21 immediately raises a crucial question about Paul's understanding of Adam. The *RSV* translates: 'Therefore as sin came into the world through one man and death through sin, and so death spread to all men because all men sinned——.' Adam sinned; this is the first premise accepted without question. Because of his disobedience, sin entered into (εἰσῆλθεν) the world. As a result of sin came death.

---

[5] In 5:1–11 it is explicit in vss. 9f.; in 5:12–21 it is explicit in vs. 21; likewise in vs. 11, at the end of 6:1–11, and in vs. 23, at the end of 6:12–23. It is found implicitly in vs. 6, at the end of 7:1–6, as well as in 24–25a at the end of 7:7–25 (assuming with many scholars that 25b is either out of order or a later gloss); the affirmation is again explicit in vs. 11 of 8:1–11 and probably in 8:39 at the end of the entire passage, since the love of God mentioned there is closely related to the spirit which brings life (cf. Rom. 5:5).

[6] What probably underlies the thinking of the cross in both these sections, as well as the one to follow (6:1–11), is Jewish martyr theology. Cf. my article, 'Romans VI.7,' *NTS*, X (1963/64), 104–108.

The end of the matter is that all men have sinned and all men die. Two problems are raised by this succession of events: 1. How does Paul solve the problem of the universality of sin? 2. How does he solve the problem of the universality of death?

Many modern commentators see nothing in verse 12 to suggest that Paul was attempting to go beyond the usual Jewish doctrine of the universality of sin. As we have seen, for contemporary Jewish theology Adam was the first sinner and the originator of sin. Paul's statement, 'Through one man sin entered into the world', would have surprised no rabbi. Paul does not even go as far as the author of IV Ezra, who attempts to explain just how Adam's sin did cause the sin of future generations. Nor does Paul say anything new about the origin of sin in Romans 5:19, which the *RSV* translates: 'For as by one man's disobedience many were made [κατεστάθησαν] sinners, so by one man's obedience many will be made righteous.' Here the issue is the contrast between the disobedience of Adam and the obedience of Christ, although controversy has centered around the correct understanding of καθίστημι. Current opinion favors the basic identification in this context of καθίστημι with γίνομαι.[7] The point is that men actually became sinners, and 19*a* should read, 'For as through the disobedience of the one man the many became sinners'. Whether or not there is also a forensic level of meaning here (that is, God *views* man as sinner) does not alter the fact that in this verse no explanation is attempted of the physical or historical relations between Adam's sin and those who followed and 'became sinners'.

I am thus led to the opinion held by some recent commentators that Paul does not have a doctrine of original sin, as the later church understood that term.[8] Barrett, for instance, concludes that 'nowhere, even in v. 19, does Paul teach the direct seminal identity between Adam and his descendants which seems to be implied in the nearly contemporary IV Ezra'.[9] Paul makes no

[7] Cf. A. Oepke, *TWNT*, III, 448; Bultmann, 'Adam and Christ according to Romans 5,' in *Current Issues in New Testament Interpretation*, eds. W. Klassen and G. Snyder (New York, 1962), p. 159.

[8] Barrett, *The Epistle to the Romans*, p. 111; Brunner, *The Letter to the Romans*, p. 44; Lietzmann, *An die Römer*, p. 61; for opposing views cf. Sanday and Headlam, *The Epistle to the Romans* (5th ed.; 'I.C.C.'; Edinburgh, 1902), p. 134; Anders Nygren, *Commentary on Romans*, (Philadelphia, 1949), p. 214; Bultmann, *Theology*, I, 251; and a strong statement by O. Kuss, *Der Römerbrief* (2d ed.; Regensburg, 1963), pp. 230–32.

[9] *Romans*, p. 111.

attempt to give a new solution to the problem of the universality of sin. Because of Adam sin has entered into history, but this judgment does not diminish each man's responsibility for his own sin. To put it another way, Adam is the necessary but not sufficient cause for the sin of other men. Paul certainly assumes everywhere that each man bears the guilt for his own acts of disobedience. This judgment is echoed in Paul's solution to the second problem: the universality of death.

Disagreement among the rabbis concerning the problem of death has already been noted.[10] According to one interpretation death was directly the result of sin. If a man did not sin, he did not die. This possibility actually was realized in the case of men such as Enoch and Elijah. The view which later became authoritative argued, on the other hand, that death was a decree given by God. All men die as a result of this decree, whether or not they sin. In this view Moses is an example; though he did not sin, he died because of the sin of Adam. In Rom. 5:12 Paul seems to give his answer to the debate.[11] He agrees with the view that death comes only as a result of individual sin. All men die *because* all men have sinned. 'Death passed through into all men, because all have sinned', ἐφ' ᾧ πάντες ἥμαρτον.[12] In I Cor. 15:56 Paul affirms that 'the sting of death is sin'. To say that sin was not counted as such until the giving of the law (Rom. 5:13) does not invalidate the point. Sin was truly in the world outside of the specific confrontation of the law. In fact this presence of sin explains why death ruled over those who were not under the law (verse 14). Death is thus universal because sin is universal; the universality of sin stems directly from each man's choice of sin and, historically, from the first such choice, that by Adam.[13]

[10] Cf. above, p. 36.

[11] A. Marmorstein also recognizes that Rom. 5 is involved in this dispute of the rabbis; cf. *ZNW*, XXX (1931), 271.

[12] It is the clear consensus of modern scholars that ἐφ'ᾧ is to be understood as 'because'.

[13] Most scholars hold that 5:12 contains an anacoluthon, the ὥσπερ clause having no true apodosis. If, however, 12*b* could be read as the apodosis, the καὶ οὕτως having the same function as οὕτως καί, which Paul usually has, then the verse would be grammatically correct and the inverted parallelism, or chiasmus, which is there in any case, would be unmistakably clear.

Therefore, just as sin entered into the world through one man, (A)
    and through sin, death, (B)
Even so death passed through into all men, (B)
    because all men have sinned. (A)

Verse 14 describes a similarity between the situation of Adam and that of Moses. 'Yet death reigned from Adam to Moses, even over those whose sins were not like the transgression of Adam, who was a type of the one who was to come.' The similarity of Adam and Moses is that both were under the Torah of God. Paul here alludes to rabbinic teaching about Adam.[14] Though the rabbis differed as to how extensive was the Torah set for Adam, there was general agreement that the first man was given specific requirements to obey. Verse 12 affirms that all men are given over to death. Verses 13f. explain what might otherwise appear incongruous, namely, that death made no distinction between those sinning under the law and those sinning without.

The only difficulty in verse 14 concerns the reference of the phrase, 'Who is a type of the coming one,' ὅς ἐστιν τύπος τοῦ μέλλοντος. Usually τοῦ μέλλοντος is taken to refer to Christ. Paul has added the phrase to prepare for the contrasts between Adam and Christ in the following verses. It must be conceded that any alternate proposal must be made quite diffidently in view of the heavy weight of scholarly consensus. Problems do arise, however, if one accepts this judgment. The most natural use of the word τύπος suggests a certain *similarity* between the figures compared. Paul nowhere gives any indication that he wants to show any positive relation between Adam and Christ. Wherever the two are juxtaposed, they are strongly contrasted.[15] Furthermore, nothing suggests that contemporary Jewish theology made any such positive link between Adam and Messiah. At most some theologians tended to relate Adam to the restoration due in the new age. Even a cursory glance at Paul convinces one that the Apostle does not accept the judgments of these theologians. In addition, the phrase, if it refers to Christ, is abruptly inserted and

---

This grammatical reading is accepted by L. Cerfaux, *Le Christ dans la theologie de Saint Paul* (Paris, 1954), p. 178, n. 1. The actual correspondence thought in the verse (a correspondence between Adam and mankind, and not a truncated one between Adam and Christ) becomes clear once the chiasmus is seen. This throws into question even more sharply Bornkamm's and Brandenburger's attempt to separate 12*d* from 12*a–c* and to derive the two sections from different thought worlds. The verse is a unity both in form and content. Cf. the discussion above, p. xixf.

[14] Cf. above, pp. 33, 42f.

[15] Bornkamm, *Ende des Gesetzes*, pp. 85–7, and Brandenburger, *Adam und Christus*, pp. 219ff., rightly emphasize the incomparability of the two figures and Paul's strongly antithetical typology.

hardly serves the purpose of the proposed transition. The contrasts which begin in verse 15 are introduced by a strong adversative, Ἀλλ' οὐχ, which serves to separate 15 from 14, not to lead out of it. Consequently I am inclined to accept a suggestion of J. A. T. Robinson that the phrase τοῦ μέλλοντος refers not to Christ but to Moses.[16] What Adam truly prefigures is Moses, since both figures were in a Torah relationship with God. This interpretation relates τοῦ μέλλοντος more naturally to its immediate context, which is a description of the period 'from Adam to Moses'. Perhaps, Robinson continues, τοῦ μέλλοντος might even refer simply to man under the law, rather than specifically to the person of Moses himself.

In verse 15 begins the great series of contrasts between Christ and Adam.[17] The transgression is compared with the gift of God in Christ. The result of the transgression is compared with the result of the gift. Overarching the whole section is the supreme contrast of life over death, separated by the 'how much more' (the *qal wḳomer*) of the side of grace and life. If it is true (and it is because this is a description of the real world) that the act of one human being wrought results of such great significance, how much more true is it that the act of another human being who at the same time is God's very act of grace could bring results of such greater import and power! Granted, Adam did cause these dire effects. But Paul can immediately shift to the 'how much more' of the other side, because God's act is 'how much more' powerful than man's. In this sense, the contrast is more between Adam and God than between Adam and Christ. Yet Christ remains central because he is God's act. Nor is the contrast primarily that between sin and righteousness, or obedience and disobedience, for we have seen that the major issue at stake throughout verses 12–21

[16] J. A. T. Robinson, *The Body: A Study in Pauline Theology* ('S.B.T.'; Chicago, 1951), p. 35.

[17] Brandenburger again seems to me incorrect in labeling vss. 15–17 as a parenthesis (*Adam und Christus*, pp. 219ff.). The point Paul has reached at the end of vs. 14 is the conclusion that every man—Gentile and Jew—sins and dies. Vss. 12–14 are really an amplification of ὄντων ἡμῶν ἀσθενῶν in 5:6 and ἁμαρτωλῶν ὄντων ἡμῶν in 5:8. Vss. 15–17 continue the thought rather than interrupt it, for what Paul now shows is that there is a man whose deed has more than offset the deed of Adam. By vs. 17 he has essentially already reached his goal: the rule of the believers in eternal life. Here is a clear progression of thought, from Adam as dead to mankind as dead, thence to Christ as victorious, and finally to the believers' reign in life.

is that of the gift of life.[18] In order to speak of death Paul has to
refer to Adam's sin; yet his major goal is to show that what lies
ahead for the believer is the restoration of life, the life which had
been God's intent for Adam. It is no accident that the section
ends in verse 21 with an exultant affirmation of the gift of eternal
life through Christ.

Verses 18f. are essentially summaries of what has already been
said, although both move forcefully in the direction the whole
section proceeds—the new life for humanity. A momentary
pause in the movement comes with verse 20. Here Torah is
mentioned to show its complete impotence, in contrast with the
act of Christ, to bring about this new life, even though it is
promised in the pages of the Torah. Many scholars have noted
that here the two great eras are those of death (Adam) and life
(Christ). The era of the law (Moses) is subordinate.[19] It would
even be more accurate to say that Torah does not represent a
separate era at all, for life under the law does not exist in some way
separate from the world of death. Paul adds that so far from bringing a new era Torah actually entrenches man in death. The Apostle
thus dethrones Moses from his position of life-giver *via* salvation
through Torah.[20] Only Jesus Christ as the life-giving Spirit (I
Cor. 15:45) enables man to participate in the kingdom of life.

I Corinthians 15

The themes of I Cor. 15 and Rom. 5:12–21 are related but not
identical. In Rom. 5 the great issue is the assurance of eternal life
through Christ. In I Cor. 15 the argument is directed, on the one
hand, towards explaining that the resurrection is a believable way
of understanding life after death and, on the other, towards
describing what the future existence will be.[21] In a very real
way the contrasts between Adam and Christ are of secondary

[18] So also Bultmann, *Theology*, I, 252.
[19] Cf. Sanday and Headlam, *Romans*, p. 143, and Althaus, *Der Brief an die
Römer*, p. 46.
[20] Cf. also II Cor. 3:7–4:6.
[21] Schmithals and others think Paul completely misunderstood the nature
of the Corinthian theology of the afterlife; cf. Schmithals, *Gnosis*, pp. 71–74.
For a critique of this view cf. my article, 'The Exaltation of the Spirit by Some
Early Christians,' *JBL*, LXXXIV (1965), 370–73. Even should Schmithals
be right, however, it does not affect our discussion here, since Paul has to be
interpreted from the standpoint of what *he* thought the issues were.

importance to each chapter. The Christology is functional; it shows what the new life is and how it is to be attained. Paul is not interested in myth-making any more than are the rabbis,[22] for both use myths to explicate the great issues of anthropology and soteriology in their faith.

The first part of I Cor. 15 is devoted to indicating the 'fact' of the resurrection of Christ and how this belief depends upon a prior faith in the resurrection of the body in general—while, conversely, the fact of Christ's resurrection supports the hope for the general resurrection. The section in which the first reference to Adam appears opens with the strong reaffirmation of Christ in his spiritual body of the resurrection (verse 20). 'Now Christ has been raised from the dead, the first fruits of those who have been sleeping.' Here is implied a fact that shall prove of decisive importance: the identity between the new body of Christ and that of the believer. Christ in his new existence is the first fruit; just as the first fruits and the main produce are the same, so the resurrection body of the redeemed in the new age will be identical with that of Christ.

Verses 21f. now make reference to the Adamic Christology in terms not unlike those of Rom. 5, with the added emphasis upon the resurrection as the form of eternal life.

21. For as by [διά] a man came death,
by a man has come also the resurrection of the dead.

22. For as in [ἐν] Adam all die,
so also in Christ shall all be made alive.

The two figures are agents. Through them have come death and life. It may be further agreed, with most critics, that πάντες in verse 22b refers or is limited to those who are in Christ, i.e., all Christians.[23] Paul clearly bases his thinking in Jewish theology about Adam as the originator of sin and death. His language is not, however, as clear as in Romans 5:12, since one could not judge from 21a and 22a whether Paul believed death was a decree by God because of Adam's sin, or whether all men died because all

---

[22] Schweitzer notes this when he says that the concept of the Last Adam in I Cor. 15 is an eschatological, not a mythical concept; *The Mysticism of Paul*, p. 167.
[23] Cf. Héring, *La Première Épître aux Corinthiens*, p. 139; Moffatt, *The First Epistle to the Corinthians*, p. 245.

men sinned. As we have seen, both alternatives were known in Jewish thought. Rom. 5:12 is surely to be taken as determinative of Paul's meaning. There, where he must spell out the relation between sin and death, he is explicit. In I Cor. 15:21f. this relation is irrelevant to what Paul wants to say, and it is understandable that he speaks less specifically.[24]

A difficult problem concerns the use of the preposition in verse 22. Is ἐν τῷ Χριστῷ to be taken in the usual Pauline sense of 'being in Christ', and is the parallel ἐν τῷ Ἀδάμ thus to be understood in some similar way?[25] Verses 21f. are probably explanatory of 20b. They intend to describe how it is that Christ is the first-fruits of the believers' resurrection. Verses 23ff. then continue the main argument. Verse 21 explains that Christ is first-fruits because through his act the resurrection of the believer not only becomes possible but has in fact taken place, just as Adam made possible and actual the death of mankind. The following verse can be taken as a parallel or epexegetical statement to the preceeding verse. In this case 'in Adam' refers to the old, or Adamic humanity and 'in Christ' refers to eschatological humanity, or more simply understood, all who believe in Christ as God's act. More probably, however, verse 22 intends to say something that goes beyond verse 21. 'If anyone is in Christ, he is a new creation' (II Cor. 5:17). Paul does not look to Christ as merely the first example of a resurrection body. Nor, as we will attempt to show later, is Christ simply the agent of the new life. Paul believes that Christ bestows upon the believer his own glorious body. Thus ἐν τῷ Χριστῷ may refer to this identity of existence—as the concept of the ἀπαρχή most surely does. By being 'in Christ' the believer will be changed to that same nature which now belongs to his Lord. Christ is then both agent (vs. 21) and pattern (vs. 22). To

---

[24] Brandenburger's attempt to deny the Jewish origin of I Cor. 15:21f. is based on two judgements. 1. Judaism had no correspondence teaching of a first and second Adam upon which Paul could draw. As we have already seen, this is quite correct. But the second argument simply cannot stand. 2. He thinks that the view of Adam as the originator of death and sin which Paul presupposes in Rom. 5:12ff. 'can scarcely have been represented by a Judaism which in any way still put the law in the middlepoint of its thinking' (*Adam und Christus*, p. 69). The evidence we have marshaled in previous chapters should demonstrate that law-abiding Jews themselves saw no discrepancy between accepting death and sin as their lot and yet finding obedience to the law as their path which led beyond death to eternal life.

[25] The uncertainties are evident in F. Neugebauer's treatment, *In Christus* (Göttingen, 1961), p. 44.

be 'in Adam' would mean analogously that man by becoming a sinner has taken upon himself the nature of the man of death.

The second statement of Adamic Christology occurs in a section (verses 35–58) which begins with the questions: 'How are the dead raised? With what kind of body do they come?' Paul is concerned primarily with a description of the nature of the resurrection body and how it differs from man's body in this age.[26] Again it should be stressed that Christology is used here only, as it were, incidentally to point to the nature of the resurrection body and to give a ground for its hope. Paul begins with an analogy taken from natural life: different bodies have different kinds of flesh (verse 39). He then shifts to the analogy of 'astronomy'; different celestial bodies differ from one another in glory (verses 40f.). The argument is that it is only natural to conceive of a body which is different from the one man now possesses. This shift from the analogy of flesh to that of heavenly glory is hardly accidental. As earlier chapters have shown, Jewish belief could view the resurrection body as possessing a glory which would equal or excel that of angels and/or heavenly bodies. Paul then (verses 42–44) contrasts the body of death with that of resurrection. By verse 44 he has arrived at a pair of contrasting terms which form both the climax and summary of his argument. 'It is sowed a physical [ψυχικόν] body; it is raised a spiritual [πνευματικόν] body.'[27] This has obviously been a planned climax because Paul uses these terms throughout the remainder of the section.

'If there is a physical body, there is also a spiritual body. Thus it is written, "The first man Adam became a living being [εἰς ψυχὴν ζῶσαν], the last Adam became a life-giving spirit" ' (44b–45).

[26] As already suggested, while σῶμα primarily means for Paul the total self, the 'I' in all its parts, in I Cor. 15 the word denotes more the form and substance of the self, although the self as willing and acting is intimately connected. The man in his new humanity is the man who wills and loves God.

[27] I give here the *RSV* translation for ψυχικόν which is probably the best that English can do. The σῶμα ψυχικόν is the distorted human existence of every man after the fall, even of the Christian, as the context of the passage makes obvious. Paul himself has a 'physical' body because he is subject to pain and death as are all other men. But in so far as the Christian is, in this world, seized by the Spirit in his inner man and made party to the knowledge and comfort the Spirit brings, Paul can contrast himself with the ψυχικὸς ἄνθρωπος, the 'unspiritual' man, and see himself as a πνευματικὸς ἄνθρωπος (I Cor. 2:14f.). Bultmann claims Paul is here using the adjective in a gnostic sense (*Theology*, I, 204), but I can see nothing in either use that would be foreign to an apocalyptic-thinking Jew who understood man apart from the eschatological gift of the Spirit to be a distorted being, ignorant of the secret counsels of God.

With these words Paul returns to the Adam-Christ contrast, now with a view to describing the respective natures of the figures. Much debate has centered around these words. Verse 44b opens with the judgment that since there is a physical body, there must also be a spiritual body. In verse 45 there is scriptural justification for this view. Gen. 2:7b is quoted as proof for the existence of physical man (a point hardly in need of proof). The difficulty arises with the words which seem to 'prove' the existence of the spiritual body. 'The last Adam became a life-giving spirit.' The argument has turned upon the question whether the sentence is taken from some now lost writing, or whether Paul is giving his own haggadic exposition of the verse in Genesis. If the latter is correct, as most scholars today think, the further problem arises as to how Paul can possibly derive a concept of the spiritual body out of Gen. 2:7. Words from this same verse appear in verse 47 of I Cor. 15, and Paul contrasts the two kinds of bodies through verse 49. He thus seems to be making a midrash on Gen. 2:7 from 44b through 49. How is this possible?

While no certain answers can be given, Paul may conceivably be giving the Corinthians a transformed version of a rabbinic discussion about Gen. 2:7 found in *Gen. R.* XIV. The issue is the *plene* spelling of the verb, 'he formed', וַיִּיצֶר, in Gen. 2:7. On the rabbinic principle that there was no unnecessary letter in Scripture the rabbis strove to find a meaning for the two *yods*, particularly in view of the fact that in verse 19, which describes the formation of beasts and birds, the same word occurs with but one *yod*. Among the various suggestions occurs the one in XIV.5.[28] The word וַיִּיצֶר denotes two formations: one is man's nature in this world and the other is his nature in the world to come. That is, Gen. 2:7 does speak of two bodies, the one the natural body, the other the resurrection body. Moreover, the context of this logion is a discussion of the nature of the resurrection body. Although it is assumed here that the body will be physical in character, the content and context of *Gen. R.* XIV.5 and I Corinthians are very similar. Paul's emphasis upon the order of the bodies, physical then spiritual, would be implicit in the rabbinic argument.

The Apostle may thus be reworking this Jewish midrash for a

[28] This logion is almost certainly early since the schools of Hillel and Shammai are connected with the context.

Greek Christian audience, although it cannot be argued that he is attempting simply to repeat it. The most acute problem is that Paul quotes the last half of the verse in Genesis while the rabbis work from the first half. Yet Paul could not explicitly reproduce for his Greek readers the midrash, since this depends upon a spelling of the Hebrew verb for its point. That Paul has the whole of the verse in his mind is indicated by I Cor. 15:47 where he refers to, or perhaps is even quoting, part of the first half of Gen. 2:7.[29] A second problem may be more apparent than real. The rabbinic logion speaks of eschatological humanity in general, while Paul appears to be specifically thinking in verse 45 of the first fruits of this humanity, the Last Adam. Certainly it is characteristic of Paul that he relates eschatological humanity to the resurrected Messiah. The whole context nevertheless makes clear that the Apostle too is thinking primarily of anthropology rather than Christology. While verse 45 does refer to the two figures as the source of the two humanities, Paul quickly shifts back in verse 46 to his basic intent, the description of the humanities themselves.

'But it is not the spiritual which is first but the physical, and then the spiritual' (verse 46). Usually Adam and Christ are thought to be the referents here. This would make Paul appear to be arguing against a view which puts the savior figure temporally prior to the figure of the earthly man. Often Philo is seen as the antithesis of Paul's position. Such an approach to the verse is surely wrong.[30] Verse 45 is an illustration or proof of verse 44. Verse 46 refers back not to verse 45 but to 44, making the subject not Adam and Christ but the nature of the two existences. Man

[29] The uncertainty stems from the difference between Paul's words and the LXX translation. Paul writes ὁ πρῶτος ἄνθρωπος ἐκ γῆς χοϊκός; the LXX translates ἄνθρωπον χοῦν ἀπὸ τῆς γῆς.

[30] The view that Paul is here arguing against a Philonic exegesis cannot be maintained. Such a view usually stems from a misunderstanding of Philo; see Addendum II below. The heavenly man of Philo is not described in Gen. 1:26f., nor does Philo ever compare the heavenly man with Adam, since the former is not a mythical figure but a platonic idea. Gen. 1:26f. and 2:7 both speak of different aspects of the creation of actual man, according to Philo, and neither of these aspects is created 'before' the other, although one part is of necessity described before the other. Gen. 1:26f. refer to the higher *nous* while Gen. 2:7 speaks either of the lower *nous* or of the complete physical nature of actual man. Paul and Philo have nothing in common with each other on this particular point. Cf. also Rawlinson, *The New Testament Doctrine of the Christ*, p. 129; Jeremias, *TWNT*, I, 143; Schweizer, *TWNT*, VI, 418.

first lives the physical existence; then he is given the spiritual body at the resurrection.

Verses 47f. are parallel in a similar way. 'The first man is from the earth, of dust; the second man is from heaven. As is the man of dust, so are those of dust; and as is the man of heaven so are those of heaven' (translation mine). The two races of men have the same nature as the originators of the races. The whole context indicates furthermore that those scholars are correct who understand the phrase in verse 47, 'the second man from heaven' (ὁ δεύτερος ἄνθρωπος ἐξ οὐρανοῦ), to refer not to the heavenly origin of Christ, nor to the second coming, but to the nature of his *resurrected* body.[31] The rabbis described physical and spiritual existence in somewhat similar ways. Angels have natures 'from above', מלמעלה. Animals have natures 'from below', מלמטן.[32] In the resurrection man will become like the angels, of a nature 'from above', although מלמעלה is not ordinarily used, as far as I know, to describe eschatological nature.[33] Paul's statements are so similar here that he may very well have had rabbinic theology in mind.

Verse 49 summarizes the whole midrash: 'Just as we have borne the image of the man of dust, let us (or: we shall) also bear the image of the man of heaven.' The believer is identified specifically with the resurrected humanity of the Messiah. Paul continually here, as well as in Rom. 5, refers to Christ in his resurrected state as ἄνθρωπος. This means, on the one hand, that no question can arise as to a possible deification of the believer through his eschatological existence, for the uniqueness of Christ as *kyrios* is nowhere compromised.[34] On the other hand it suggests Paul's main concern with his Adamic Christology, to speak of the believer's future human existence. The parallelism in verse 49 speaks also against any attempt to water down the identity between Christ and believer which would affirm that the believer will possess only a reflection of Christ's resurrected glory. To bear the

[31] So Moffatt, *The First Epistle to the Corinthians*, p. 263; Weiss, *Der erste Korintherbrief*, p. 376. Wilhelm Michaelis agrees and adds that the phrase denotes the 'Qualifikation des Erhöhten, der vom Himmel' ist, weil er den 'pneumatischen Leib' trägt'; *Zur Engelchristologie im Urchristentum* (Basel, 1942), p. 42.

[32] *Gen. R.* VIII.11; cf. also Philo, *Op. mundi* 46; II Enoch 30:8–10.

[33] But cf. *Gen. R.* XXI.1.

[34] Perhaps it is instructive to note that in verse 47 Marcion replaced ἄνθρωπος as a reference to Christ with κύριος. He apparently was scandalized by the idea that Christ in his exaltation could still be called man.

image of the man of dust means to exist in the same nature as the fallen Adam; to bear the image of the man of heaven must be understood in a similar manner.[35] To exist in a spiritual body also means to be a man who bears the powers and fruits of the Spirit, that is, to be a man perfectly related to God and neighbor. This would have been self-apparent to Paul. There is little doubt, however, that he, as his Jewish contemporaries, speaks of the resurrection body in terms of its nature, not its ethics, and that in I Cor. 15 he is primarily concerned with this nature.

The First Adam

The evidence for Paul's view of the first Adam may now be collected and assessed. The amount of this evidence is perhaps surprisingly small. Just as Paul is more interested in the new creation than in the old, so he says more about the Last Adam than the first. Adam was the first sinner, and his sin was a sin against God's Torah. Thus the 'likeness of the sin of Adam', that is, the actual quality of Adam's sin, is identical with the quality of those later sins against the law of God given to Moses. Paul speaks of Adam's deed in Romans 5:15 as a παράπτωμα, which means a transgression against a definite law. As a result the sin of Adam is disobedience, παρακοή (verse 19). Adam refused to take upon himself the yoke of Torah and rebelled against God. Doubtless, Paul might agree that what he says about man's sin in general could be applied to the first sin; in the face of a lack of positive evidence, however, it is illegitimate to make such a transfer.[36]

A hint of Paul's judgment upon Adam may be gleaned from Philippians 2:5–11. While the subtlety of the allusions in this passage defies positive identification, many scholars have argued

[35]A minor question in verse 49b concerns the mood of φορέω. A great majority of the important witnesses read the subjunctive, 'Let us bear.' In spite of this a majority of scholars prefer the future as attested by Vaticanus and Freer. While the future perhaps fits more easily the context of I Cor. 15, it is not easy to override the preponderance of good texts which read the subjunctive, particularly in view of the fact that the idea it conveys is Pauline (cf. Rom. 12:2, II Cor. 4:16, and Col. 3:10). Consequently some scholars do take the subjunctive as correct, and it perhaps could be accepted as the *lectio difficilior.* Cf. Héring, *Corinthiens,* p. 149, and Allo, *Corinthiens,* p. 429.

[36] That Paul is thinking of Genesis 3 in Rom. 7:11 seems to me doubtful, but cf. Davies, *Paul and Rabbinic Judaism,* p. 32. I have already argued against seeing a reference to Adam's sin in Rom. 1:23.

H

that behind the obedient service of Christ lies a contrast with the disobedient self-assertion of Adam.[37] The key to this interpretation is verse 6, which many interpreters today take to mean, 'who being in the form of God did not count equality with God a thing to be grasped'. The passage then contrasts this possible attitude of grasping with the self-emptying of Christ in the Incarnation. Christ thus may be compared with Adam who did eat of the fruit of the tree, hoping to become like the gods. Other contrasts have also been suggested, such as that between Christ and Satan. The difficulty is, of course, that these verses are likely a pre-Pauline hymn; thus reasoning from what Paul says elsewhere to this passage is not without its difficulties.[38] Furthermore Paul nowhere else suggests that man covets divinity. To say more than that an Adamic allusion possibly *may* be found in Philippians 2 is unwarranted.[39]

Through Adam sin entered into the world. While Paul has no doctrine of original sin, he does describe the first sin as the origin of all human sin in history. All men in fact do sin and thus become guilty of death. Man thus enters into judgment, κρίμα, and because of guilt is led to condemnation, κατάκριμα (Rom. 5:16). Because of κατάκριμα death rules. Death is here seen not as a once-for-all decision rendered by God at the occasion of the first sin, but as related directly to each man's sinfulness. Probably Paul is thinking in Rom. 5:16f. directly upon the narrative in Gen. 3, where Adam and Eve are judged, condemned, and sentenced to death. If Paul has a belief in a general resurrection of wicked as well as righteous, he may also have in mind the scene of the future judgment.[40] Curiously enough, Paul never says that Adam caused the loss of the glory and image which God intended for man, although he clearly knows man now lacks these and can only

[37] So Cullmann, *Christology of the New Testament*, pp. 174–81; P. Bonnard, *L'Épître de Saint Paul aux Philippiens* ('C.N.T.'; Neuchatel, 1950), p. 43; Ch. Guignebert, 'Quelques remarques d'exégèse sur Philippiens, 2, 6–11,' *RHPR*, III (1923), 522f.; also examples of earlier opinions in M. R. Vincent, *Epistle to the Philippians and to Philemon* ('I.C.C.'; New York, 1897), pp. 84f., though Vincent himself rejects such an interpretation.

[38] But cf. Davies, *Paul and Rabbinic Judaism*, pp. 41f.

[39] Nor is it clear to me that the best interpretation of ἁρπαγμός in vs. 6 is the *res rapienda* necessary to the interpretation. The *res rapta* (a prize already possessed) perhaps fits the context of the hymn better; cf. Käsemann, 'Kritische Analyse von Phil. 2, 5–11,' in *Exegetische Versuche und Besinnungen*, I (Göttingen, 1964), 69–71.

[40] Cf. the discussion of I Cor. 15:20–28 in the commentaries *ad loc.*

possess them through the gift of the resurrection. The Apostle is consistently silent about Adam's status prior to his sin. The reason for this must be, as will be shown, that Paul knows only Christ as the exhibition of God's intent for man and thus has nothing to say about what Adam was before the fall or might have been had he not sinned.

The sin of Adam has led to the corruption of the whole cosmos (Rom. 8:18–22). Again Paul seems to follow quite simply the Genesis narrative as it was interpreted by Jewish theologians. 'For the creation was subjected to futility, not of its own will but by the will of him who subjected it in hope' (Rom. 8:20). The creation was subjected to futility, ματαιότης; this is a contrasting term to τέλος and here denotes failure to reach a goal set for creation.[41] Thus the cosmos lacks the glory of God as does man. It was subjected by God, for God cursed the ground because of man.[42] The original paradise has disappeared and the world doomed to corruption and decay.

Thus Paul's picture of Adam is consistent with the narrative in Gen. 3. Almost every major concern of the Yahwist is mentioned in the Epistles. Paul's understanding also follows closely that part of Jewish treatment of Adam which saw in the first man the origin of sin and death. But now it becomes obvious that the Apostle has nothing at all to do with the other side of Jewish exegesis, where Adam is by some means exonerated of his sin, becomes the first patriarch, and is the person who exhibits the portrait of and assurance for man's eschatological existence. This absence of such an important part of Jewish teaching would be startling except for one decisive fact: Christ as Last Adam now plays the role of the portrait and assurance of eschatological humanity. He becomes, furthermore, the means by which the new humanity is attained, a feature Jewish theology never ascribed to Adam. The unique feature of Paul's Adamic Christology then lies precisely in the shift of these important theological functions from the first Adam to the Last. To this Christology we now turn.

[41] Sanday and Headlam, *Romans*, p. 207.
[42] Cf. the rabbinic maxim: 'Three entered into judgment but four came out cursed', j*Kil*.I.7,27*b*.

The Last Adam

The resurrection of Christ is a central motif in Paul's theology. This emphasis becomes even clearer when Paul is compared with someone like the author of Hebrews, who does not display much interest in the resurrection. The reason for Paul's stress on the resurrection of Christ is not, however, as certain. Perhaps there is too great a tendency to read into Paul the reasons of later Christian apologetics. Is the *fact* of Christ's resurrection emphasized in order to bolster hope for the resurrection of Christians? Such a desire may be present in Paul, but his basic motivation is not found here. In I Cor. 15, for example, the beliefs in the general resurrection and in Christ's resurrection are mutually supporting. That is, Paul can argue from faith in the general resurrection to the fact of its particular manifestation in Christ, as well as *vice versa*. For Paul, as for most Pharisaic Jews, belief in the resurrection, at least of the faithful, had become virtually an assured fact.

The reason for the Apostle's stress on Christ's resurrection is based, rather, on his belief that the resurrection marks the beginning of the humanity of the Last Adam. Christ has become the model and means of the resurrection of the Christian. In his body of glory Christ is true humanity, the realization of that existence the Christian will himself have one day. Christ is also the mediator of that nature. Thus the resurrection of Christ does not function for Paul so much to 'prove' the resurrection in general as to give assurance to the Christian just what kind of existence is to be his and how it is to be obtained. In other words, Paul now knows that it is Christ, not Adam, who assures man of his eschatological humanity.

The New Testament church does not agree about the nature of Christ's resurrected body. Material in Luke and John perhaps suggests this body to be corporeal in nature.[43] Paul, on the other hand, clearly argues that the body is a spiritual body. If any historical memory resides in the accounts of Paul's conversion in Acts, he must not have understood the appearance of Christ to have been a corporeal appearance. Most critics identify this conversion with the event referred to in I Cor. 15:8: 'Last of all,

---

[43] Luke 24:39–43; John 20:26–38. There are, of course, contradictory elements in the stories which imply the body is more than physical.

as to one untimely born, he appeared also to me.'[44] The arguments
in verses 47–50 of this chapter for the identity between Christ's
body and the spiritual body of the resurrection indicate that for
the Apostle his Lord rose from the dead in a spiritual body. Most
importantly, Paul has equated the appearance of Christ to him
with the appearances to other apostles. The resurrected Christ, as
he was manifested to the church, is thus a spiritual body. The
task must now be to search out how Paul otherwise describes the
existence of the risen Christ and to see how this description is
related to his belief about eschatological man.

1. The nature of Christ's resurrected existence is a *human*
nature. In I Cor. 15:21 this belief is clearly stated. 'For as by a
man came death, by a man has come also the resurrection of the
dead.' Paul probably has more than the earthly existence of
Jesus in mind, since he speaks of Christ in his resurrected nature
as ἄνθρωπος. 'Just as we have borne the image of the man of dust,
we shall also bear the image of the man of heaven', τὴν εἰκόνα τοῦ
ἐπουρανίου [ἀνθρώπου] (verse 49). Verse 47 duplicates the idea:
'The second man is from heaven.' Christ even in his exalted
nature is ἄνθρωπος. The humanity is also stressed in Rom. 5.
Made explicit in verse 15, the contrast between the two men is
implied throughout the remainder of the passage. 'But the free
gift is not like the trespass. For if many died through one man's
trespass, much more have the grace of God and the free gift in the
grace of that one man Jesus Christ abounded for many.' Here it is
true that the aorist might imply that the cross of Jesus is in mind.
In verse 17, however, the tense is future. The gift of eternal life is
still a future event to be bestowed by the man Jesus Christ, διὰ
τοῦ ἑνὸς [ἀνθρώπου] Ἰησοῦ Χριστοῦ.[45]

Paul is not describing here the earthly Jesus. In so far as he
mentions Jesus' earthly life elsewhere (Rom. 8:3 and Phil. 2:7f.),
he appears to identify the nature of Jesus with that of other men.
Jesus has come in the likeness of sinful flesh, ἐν ὁμοιώματι σαρκὸς
ἁμαρτίας (Rom. 8:3). But Christ by virtue of his resurrection is
not changed from being a man; he is rather changed *into* the true
man. While the two natures—earthly and exalted—differ radically

[44] Cf., e.g., Robertson and Plummer, *The First Epistle to the Corinthians*,
p. 340; cf. also Gal. 1:16.
[45] The omission of the word ἄνθρωπος in this verse and in I Cor. 15:49 is
not significant. It is due to stylistic reasons.

in their existence, both are nevertheless human natures. The very fact that Christ is 'first-born of many brethren' is an indication of his continuing humanity. Paul uses this phrase in Romans 8:29 and it is echoed in Col. 1:18. Πρωτότοκος, 'first-born', may here bear the emphasis of a priority of value rather than of time, but the reference to other brethren implies a close kinship between Christ and the redeemed. Both are related by their essential humanity.

2. But Christ as man is the man *from heaven*. The precise meaning of ἐξ οὐρανοῦ in I Cor. 15:47 has been hotly debated. I have argued that the context demands that ἐξ οὐρανοῦ refer primarily to the nature of the humanity of Christ (and of the Christian). Paul contrasts the earthly nature of the first man with the non-corporeal nature of the eschatological man, a nature which is probably to be seen as like that of the angels. The antonymous pairs, natural-spiritual, earthly-heavenly, corruptible-incorruptible, all point to the same contrast, that the nature of Christ's resurrected body is of a heavenly 'substance', or to use Paul's term, σῶμα. After repeated attempts to put into analogies what is essentially non-analogical, Paul sums up his intent in the following words, which are permeated with Jewish terminology: 'This I say, brethren, because (or that) flesh and blood are not able to inherit God's kingdom.'[46] Formally Paul's arguments represent one side of the debate within Jewish theology concerning the nature of eschatological man. What is Christian about the argument is that Paul is now able to look to present reality—to Christ —to base his hopes for a spiritual body.

3. Closely connected with the above is Paul's use of πνεῦμα and πνευματικός in his Adamic Christology. He does not choose to say directly that Christ now possesses a spiritual body; Christ is, rather, the Spirit which creates life (I Cor. 15:45). Nevertheless, there can be no doubt that Paul assumes Christ does exist in a spiritual σῶμα. As a result of the life-giving πνεῦμα, the believer will also possess a spiritual body. We have already seen that the Spirit influences the entire man. The Spirit relates to God's life in man, to the power which enables man to live in right relation to God and man, and to the communication of wisdom and insight into God's intent for human existence. Thus in I Cor. 15 Christ

---

[46] I Cor. 15:50, trans. mine.

as πνεῦμα refers primarily to his role as agent of the new creation. The application of πνευματικός to σῶμα probably then refers both to the non-corporeal, spiritual nature of the σῶμα, somewhat parallel to the word οὐράνιος, as well as to the source of this σῶμα, the life-giving Spirit. Rom. 8:11 also relates eschatological existence to the Spirit, although in this verse Paul has God in mind as the source of the Spirit rather than Christ. 'If the Spirit of him who raised Jesus from the dead dwells in you, he who raised Christ Jesus from the dead will give life to your mortal bodies also through his Spirit which dwells in you.' The difference between this verse and I Cor. 15:45 is that the latter depicts Christ as the mediator of the πνεῦμα, for Christ *is* the πνεῦμα.[47]

In so far as the πνεῦμα is the presupposition of a genuine life in relation to neighbor and God, Christ is the bestower of these gifts as well. Though nothing explicitly is said to the point here, the renewal or new creation of man in his total existence, moral, religious, as well as bodily, is at stake. Paul, of course, would never feel it necessary to speak about the religious and ethical posture of the exalted Christ in the same way as he spoke of that of the earthly Jesus. Nor is he concerned to expound on such a posture for man in heaven. Doubtless eschatological man in his heavenly existence is perfect, but who would need to belabor such an obvious point? Paul is thinking of the nature of man's body in the new age, but he would be aghast if someone suggested to him that he was thus ignoring the decisional or ethical aspects of his faith. All these are implied in the concept of Christ as life-giving πνεῦμα.

4. Christ is the glory of God. That Christ manifests God's glory is an idea common to Paul and the New Testament in general. At times Christ as δόξα is the revelation of God's δόξα. At least this is partly the case in II Cor. 3:7–4:6, where Moses is contrasted with the superior revelation or glory of Christ. Yet in Paul most references to Christ's glory either describe the glorious nature of the exalted Lord or assure the Christian that he will receive the glory which Christ now has. In Rom. 8:17 Paul exhorts Christians to suffer with Christ in order that they may also be glorified with him. Phil. 3:20f. contains the same idea. The body of glory which Christ has is mentioned only to indicate that

[47] Cf. also II Cor. 3:17, where the gift of the eschatological existence is also related to Christ as the πνεῦμα.

Christ will change the bodies of Christians to be like his. Likewise, Col. 3:4 suggests that 'when Christ who is our life appears, then you also will appear with him in glory'. Paul even in II Cor. 3:7–4:6 is not content to depict Christ's glory as revelatory. His nature is glorious and it will be given to man. 'And we all, with unveiled face, beholding the glory of the Lord, are being changed into his likeness from one degree of glory to another; for this comes from the Lord who is the Spirit' (II Cor. 3:18). True, the glory of Christ reveals to us God's decision for man; but true too is that man is to be transformed into this glory.

An allusion probably occurs in II Cor. 4:6 to Paul's Adamic Christology. 'For it is the God who said, "Let light shine out of darkness", who has shone in our hearts to give the light of knowledge of the glory of God in the face of Christ.' As we have seen, the rabbis held that the original countenance of Adam was exceedingly brilliant in glory, such that it outshone the sun. One Tannaitic tradition held that since the ball of Adam's heel outshone the sun, how much more did his face.[48] The Corinthian passage as a whole reflects the contrast between Moses and Christ. Nevertheless, Paul's mind is turned by his description of Christ's glory to the motif of creation. He refers in 4:4 to Christ as the image of God and in 4:6 to God's command at the beginning of creation. Paul seems at this point to have transferred to Christ the rabbinic idea of Adam's original brilliance.[49] Again the Apostle has given the exalted Christ a trait his Jewish contemporaries applied to Adam before the fall. The true glory of man is to be found not in looking back to the old creation, but to the new creation as it has dawned in Christ.

In sum, Paul knows that his Lord possesses an exalted nature of glory. His glory is that intended by God for man at creation, now revealed and realized at the new creation. The end result will be that Christ 'will change our lowly body to be like his glorious body' (Phil. 3:21).

[48] E.g., Simon b. Menasya; cf. *Tanh. B.*, *ḥuqot* 17 (57b).

[49] So also M. Black, 'The Pauline Doctrine of the Second Adam,' *SJT*, VII (1954), 174. It is also possible, as Davies suggests, that the light of the face of Christ refers to the original light created by God in Gen. 1:3; cf. *Paul and Rabbinic Judaism*, p. 37. This original light would then most likely be not the sun but that light created prior to and far more brilliant than the sun, and taken from the world because of Adam's sin. It is to be restored in the messianic age; cf. *Gen. R.* XII.6.

5. Christ is the image of God. This motif is explicitly stated in two places, II Cor. 4:4 and Col. 1:15, and probably implied in others. The main problem here concerns whether or not εἰκών in these passages is related to Gen. 1. F. W. Eltester argues that in Paul, as in Philo, the idea has its roots in the *sophia* and *Urmensch* speculation of Hellenistic Judaism.[50] Any relation with Gen. 1 is contrived because Scripture is used only as a means of supporting an already evolved and accepted concept.[51] To this several things can be said. (*a*) Whatever its origin *sophia* speculation had been accepted also by Palestinian Judaism, so that there is no necessity to look only to Hellenism for the source of Paul's language. (*b*) The crucial determination here as always is not the origins but the use of the concept. To prove that εἰκών originated in Hellenism does not necessarily indicate what Paul intended to say. (*c*) The context thus must finally decide the meaning of Paul's use—and this means not only the immediate passage but his entire theological viewpoint as well. On both counts a direct relation with Gen. 1 is difficult to deny. II Cor. 4:6 is clearly a midrash on Gen. 1, with its allusion to the Adamic concept, and is closely tied to verse 4, in which εἰκών occurs. Jervell in fact believes the entire section, II Cor. 3:18–4:6, to be a midrash on Gen. 1:27.[52] Col. 1:15 is also concerned with the events of creation. Christ is not only εἰκὼν τοῦ θεοῦ, as was Adam, but also king over creation in a way vastly different from the first man. Eltester is correct in arguing that the cosmic role of Christ in Col. 1:15ff. cannot be derived from Gen. 1:27 alone.[53] What has first to be proven, however, is that a cosmic role is implied in Paul's use of the *specific* phrase, εἰκὼν τοῦ θεοῦ, and this is not forthcoming. As so often happens, it is the person of Christ, not a single term, which unites the various motifs. According to F. W. Beare, Col. 1:15f. is related to all of Gen. 1, not simply to verse 27.[54] In the opening chapter of the Bible, ideas of creation, sovereignty, and divine image all appear, and these are the very motifs found in the passage in Colossians. 'Thus he [Jesus] is the embodiment of true humanity, as he is the embodiment of true kingship.'[55] Furthermore, the context of Paul's whole theology indicates that the

---

[50] F. W. Eltester, *Eikon im Neuen Testament* (Berlin, 1958), pp. 130–40.
[51] Ibid., p. 148.   [52] *Imago Dei*, p. 174.   [53] *Eikon*, p. 148.
[54] *IB*, XI, 164.   [55] Ibid.

Apostle wrestles mightily with Gen. 1-3.[56] The very fact that the Adamic theology occupies a prominent place in his thinking is enough to give pause to attempts to direct the εἰκών concept elsewhere. Thus, whatever the source for the phrase, Paul relates it to Gen. 1 and intends it, I believe, to be understood within the general framework of the biblical passage. This is the position held today by many scholars.[57]

When Paul relates the concept of εἰκών to Gen. 1, he suggests that Christ is the reality of true humanity. My argument that the Christian by being transformed into this image becomes true man supports such an interpretation, at least indirectly.[58] The passages in Colossians and II Corinthians, however, do contain an apparent difficulty. In both instances Christ as εἰκών is the revelation of God. In II Cor. 4:6 the radiance of Christ's face is God's glory. Col. 1:15 seems to emphasize that Christ is the 'visible' image of the invisible God. Jervell, thus impressed, refuses to allow any reference here to the true humanity found in the exalted Christ. As εἰκών Christ is rather the revelation of divinity.[59]

The startling answer to this difficulty is that, for Paul as well as for Gen. 1, both meanings of εἰκών hold at the same time. Christ is the true revelation of God *precisely because* he is true man. The reverse is equally true. In Gen. 1 man, as εἰκών τοῦ θεοῦ, is that being who is most like God and who exercises God's vice-regency on earth. Jewish theology understood this when it claimed that before his fall Adam manifested glory, a glory originating, however, not with him but with God. Paul now knows Christ to be true man, and this means that Christ is the image and glory *of God*.[60] To see God one looks to Christ; thus the true humanity now realized in Christ is the true revelation of God. Paul has taken up the radical emphasis of Judaism upon the

---

[56] For a collection and discussion of Pauline texts related to the early chapters of Genesis, cf. Wilhelm Dittmann, 'Die Auslegung der Urgeschichte (Gen. 1-3) im Neuen Testament' (microfilmed doctoral dissertation; Göttingen, 1953), pp. 157ff.

[57] *TWNT*, II, 394; Lietzmann, *Korinther*, p. 115; Windisch, *Der zweite Korintherbrief*, p. 137; Beare, *IB*, XI, 164; Masson, *Colossiens*, p. 98; Jervell, *Imago Dei*, p. 174; C. F. Burney, 'Christ as the ARXH of Creation,' *JTS*, XXVII (1926), 160.

[58] Cf. above, pp. 00.

[59] Jervell, *Imago Dei*, pp. 214ff.

[60] The hope for eternal life which is the theme of Rom. 5-8 is defined at the very beginning by Paul as the hope for the glory *of God* (Rom. 5:2).

theomorphism of man. No hesitation need exist in understanding εἰκὼν τοῦ θεοῦ to be an affirmation by Paul that his Lord *is* the regained humanity God intended to exist at creation.

Christ as image is also implied in other passages. This is certainly the case with II Cor. 3:18. 'And we all, with unveiled face, beholding the glory of the Lord, are being changed into the same image from one degree of glory to another, for this comes from the Lord who is the Spirit.' Here it is clear that δόξα and εἰκών are practically synonymous. Man is to be changed not into an image of Christ but rather into that image of God which is now the nature of Christ. Thus 'the same image', equatable here with 'glory of the Lord', refers to Christ as the image of God. Earlier we argued that Rom. 8:29 carries a similar nuance; here the believer is to be 'conformed to the image which the son is.'[61] Christ as image of God clearly describes eschatological humanity. This image, now visible completely only in Christ, will one day be given to the believer.

Christ is man, first-born of many brethren, man of heaven, the life-giving Spirit, the glory and image of God. These are the motifs Paul uses to relate his Lord to the new creation, and they are all summed up in the title, the Last Adam, ὁ ἔσχατος ʼΑδάμ. Do these motifs help us to understand the function which the whole complex of the Adamic Christology has for Paul? To put the question more acutely: Why does Paul attempt to relate Adam and Christ? What does he express in this relation that he could not as well accomplish by other language? One danger of a motif study is that it may become too inclusive, that what Paul says generally of Christ may too easily be related to the particular motif in question. Thus it is necessary to exclude unrelated or tangential motifs which might obscure the basic function of Christ as Last Adam. One contrast Paul draws between Adam and Christ is that of their inner motivation or relationship to God. Adam was disobedient; Christ, obedient. Perhaps, if Phil. 2:5–11 applies, Paul further suggests that Adam grasped at what did not belong to him, while Christ surrendered his rightful prerogatives to become a servant. Yet this cannot be sufficient cause for the whole construction Paul builds around the theme of Adam. The Adamic

[61] Cf. also E. Larsson, *Christus als Vorbild* (Lund, 1962), pp. 302–305. Larsson, however, accepts the *Urbild/Abbild* distinction between Christ and believer upon which Jervell insists.

Christology speaks of the exalted Lord, not the historical activity of Jesus. A second tangential motif contrasts one of the results of their acts: Adam brought sin to the world, while Christ was the expiation for sin. Paul, however, does not emphasize this contrast. When he writes directly of the atonement and its effects he uses other motifs.[62] Even in Rom. 5 the issues of sin and expiation are not central.[63]

CHRIST AS THE REALIZATION OF TRUE HUMANITY

Paul uses his Adamic Christology for two central purposes, which he finds easiest to carry out by means of this specific language. The first is signaled by the contrast between the humanity of Adam and that of Christ. Everything said so far has pointed toward this conclusion. It is for no casual purpose that Paul transfers the Jewish ascriptions of Adam's excellence before the fall to Christ. Nowhere in the Epistles is Adam the perfect man before his sin. Paul knows only the Adam of sin and death. Where does Paul look to find man's true nature? He now looks to Christ. The resurrected and exalted Christ is the perfect realization of God's intent for man. Man no longer has to look to what once was but is now no longer; he can acknowledge the reality of God's promise in his Messiah and Lord. Jewish theology paid much attention to the portrait of man in his original perfection. There is no reason to doubt that Paul too felt a pressing need to know God's design for man. Just in his Adamic Christology Paul finds the answer. The Apostle, moreover, rejoices in the firm assurance that his faith is in present reality. He has seen Christ; the true man now lives eternally in the heavens. 'But thanks be to God, who gives us the victory through our Lord Jesus Christ.'

Biblical interpreters have occasionally suggested this as one function of Paul's Christology,[64] although their exegetical basis

---

[62] The sacrificial motif is prominent and perhaps also that of the righteous martyr. Cf. Davies, *Paul and Rabbinic Judaism*, pp. 230–84; Schoeps, *Paul* (Philadelphia, 1961), pp. 126–49; Scroggs, *NTS*, X (1963/64), 104–108.

[63] It is interesting to note that in rabbinic thought, atonement, forgiveness, or penitence play no part whenever the restoration of Adam's nature is being discussed. The Adamic theology of the rabbis thus has the same general limitations as does that of Paul.

[64] E.g., Jean Héring, 'Kyrios Anthropos,' *RHPR*, XVI (1936), 205; cf. also a further treatment, with exploration of some theological consequences, in his 'Les Bases bibliques de l'humanisme chrétien,' *RHPR*, XXV (1945), 17ff.; Althaus, *Römer*, pp. 47f.; Beare, *IB*, XI, 164; Masson, *Colossiens*, p. 98; Windisch, *Der zweite Korintherbrief*, p. 137.

has not always been adequate. Yet it has been left to Karl Barth to state the issues most explicitly.[65] Barth argues that for Paul the anthropology of Christ is primary and prior to that of Adam. The special anthropology of Christ is the norm of all anthropology, while Adam in his humanity merely 'pre-figures' that of Christ.[66] It is not the case that Adam's humanity is the natural one, while that of Christ provides something essentially unnatural. 'Our relationship to Adam depends for its reality on our relationship to Christ. And that means, in practice, that to find the true and essential nature of man we have to look not to Adam the fallen man, but to Christ in whom what is fallen has been cancelled and what was original has been restored.'[67] Whether or not Barth has accurately derived these ideas from Rom. 5 alone, what he says reflects Paul's general position. The humanity of Christ is prior to that of Adam in the sense that God's intent for man is prior to Adam's rebellion. Paul, of course, thinks of the Last Adam only as an eschatological reality, so that the question of a temporal priority does not arise. *Seen from the vantage point of the new creation*, Adam's humanity is indeed a derived, distorted humanity.

A final point must be made. We have already argued that Christ is the Last Adam in his resurrected body.[68] This means that for Paul Christ is and remains man after his resurrection. He is, of course, the man in the image of God and therefore closely related to God himself. But far from implying that Christ loses his humanity and becomes a non-human divine form, Paul's view of the Last Adam is indebted to his Jewish heritage, which believed that eschatological man would be superior to every form of being except Yahweh himself. Thus the closeness of Christ to God's form does not argue against his essential humanity; rather it is proof that he is, in fact, resurrected *man*. A word which Behm wrote about the Old Testament holds true for the eschatological anthropology of Judaism and Paul. 'In the Old Testament the

[65] Karl Barth, *Christ and Adam*. All of Barth's exegesis may not be accurate, as Bultmann notes in his reply to Barth in *Current Issues in New Testament Interpretation*, pp. 143–165. Nevertheless, Barth seems to me to be correct in his general conclusions.

[66] Barth, *Christ and Adam*, p. 5.   [67] Ibid., p. 24.

[68] So also Schweitzer, *The Mysticism of Paul*, p. 167; K. H. Rengstorf, *Die Auferstehung Jesu* (Witten, Ruhr, 1954), p. 73; Michaelis, *Engelchristologie*, p. 42.

theomorphic understanding of man is more essential than the anthropomorphic conceptions of God.'[69]

This now enables us to return to a question raised at the beginning of the study. Why is Christ in his exalted state called ἄνθρωπος? Is it necessary to think that Paul has in mind the motif of the Son of Man, although he never explicitly mentions this concept? If my argument is correct, the title 'Man' is to be explained rather as belonging inherently to Paul's *Adamic* Christology. Only if Christ *is* man can Paul see and be assured of that true humanity which is the intent of God's creativity. Care must be taken not to modernize what Paul means when he speaks of true humanity. For him to describe the exalted Christ as the perfect religious man would be pointless. To say that Paul is concerned with the nature of eschatological humanity does not exclude, of course, the assumption that this nature is of an ethically and religiously perfected man; but it does suggest that Paul's main desire is to depict that nature in which such perfection may exist. To translate Paul's Adamic Christology into primarily ethical categories is both a reduction and a distortion of Paul's intent, however important such a translation may seem to be for contemporary theology.

CHRIST AS THE MEDIATOR OF TRUE HUMANITY

Important as is the first function of Paul's Adamic Christology, the second is almost more crucial, since it is at the center of God's promise to men. In Jewish theology the Messiah is only in the most general way connected with the life in the new age. In the rabbinic logion mentioned frequently above, the restoration of man is related to the days of the Messiah, not to the Messiah himself (*Gen. R.* XII 6). That the Messiah might have an active role in the process of rejuvenation is the exception rather than the rule.[70] Paul strikes a new note: Christ not only is true humanity; he also mediates this true humanity to the believer. Paul's description of the future existence of Christians parallels, as we have seen, that of the exalted Christ. Both are to possess glory, eternal life, a spiritual or heavenly body, and God's image. Given this relationship, the problem is how it is to be explained and how obtained.

[69] *TWNT*, IV, 756.   [70] T. Levi 18 is such an exception.

Both of the central Adamic passages describe Christ as the agent of life. It is by or through (διά) Christ that life reigns or that the believer will live eternally. Life, ζωή, is the term which encompasses all of the new humanity. When one has eternal life he has that existence originally intended by God and now given as a gift. In Col. 3:4 Christ is even called 'our life'. So far this is the common kerygma of the New Testament, for almost all the writings affirm the centrality of Christ, in one way or another, for eternal life. Paul's writing, however, displays an intensity at this point which goes far beyond the formal proclamation.

According to Phil. 3:21 Christ 'will change our lowly body to be like his glorious body, by the power which enables him even to subject all things to himself', ὃς μετασχηματίσει τὸ σῶμα τῆς ταπεινώσεως ἡμῶν σύμμορφον τῷ σώματι τῆς δόξης αὐτοῦ. Μετασχηματίζω in this context means to change the external form or fashion of the nature of man, just as Paul elsewhere says that the σχῆμα of the world is passing away (I Cor. 7:31). The word μορφή can denote either the external manifestation, or the true inner being of a thing.[71] The compound, σύμμορφος, suggests here that the eschatological nature of the believer will be identical in respect of its μορφή with that of the resurrected Christ.[72] Thus whether μορφή means manifestation or essence is not crucial to the argument, because everything hinges on the identity of Christ and believer rather than on the exact content of the μορφή. Furthermore, the verse explains how this marvelous change is to be wrought—by the unique and complete power which God has given Christ over all things.

While in Phil. 3:21 the believer is to be conformed to Christ's glory, in Rom. 8:29 he is to be conformed to Christ's image. 'For those whom he foreknew he also predestined to be conformed [σύμμορφον] to the image of his Son, in order that he might be the first-born among many brethren.' Lietzmann is surely correct here in arguing that the term εἰκών refers to the exalted body of the resurrection.[73] The believer will come to possess that very

---

[71] Behm argues for the meaning of external characteristics, *TWNT*, IV, 753ff., Dibelius for the meaning, 'essence,' in Philippians, cf. *An die Thessalonicher I.II An die Philipper* (3d. ed.; 'H.N.T.'; Tübingen, 1937), p. 74, as does Vincent, *Philippians and Philemon*, p. 57.

[72] Cf. Bonnard, *Philippiens*, p. 72.

[73] *Römer*, p. 87.

image of God which Christ now possesses as the resurrected Lord. The passage is reminiscent of I Cor. 15:49: 'Just as we have borne the image of the man of dust, let us also bear the image of the man of heaven.' Man will have a body which is identical with that of the Last Adam, just as he is now burdened with a body identical with that of the first Adam. Since the concepts of image and glory are virtually synonymous, the verses in Philippians, Romans, and I Corinthians differ little if at all in content from one another.

Important in Rom. 8:29 is the phrase, 'first-born of many brethren'. πρωτότοκος often implies a priority of rank. Probably such is the case here, but the emphasis of Paul lies rather in the similarity of form.[74] God's determination to make the believer conform to the image of Christ results in Christ's becoming the first-born. Paul once again uses πρωτότοκος in Col. 1:18. Christ is 'first-born from the dead'. Here the word is linked directly with the resurrection body. Christ's resurrection is the beginning point which culminates in similar resurrections among the believers.[75] Probably similar in meaning to πρωτότοκος is the concept of first fruits in I Cor. 15:20.[76] The relation between the body of the resurrected Christ and the future bodies of believers is likened to that between the produce offered as sacrifice and the same kind of produce which may afterward be eaten. The assumption underlying the metaphor is the identity between the natures.

Two other passages in Paul support the above argument. In Rom. 8:17 Paul stresses the similarity between Christ and the eschatological Christian. Believers are children of God, that is, 'heirs of God and fellow heirs with Christ, provided we suffer with him in order that we may also be glorified with him'. Here the prefix συν- is used three times to emphasize the relationship between Christ and believer. Κληρονόμοι μὲν θεοῦ, συγκληρονόμοι δὲ Χριστοῦ, εἴπερ συμπάσχομεν ἵνα καὶ συνδοξασθῶμεν. The glorification refers to the body of glory, as Phil. 3:21 indicates. Col. 3:4 says essentially the same thing. When Christ is manifested, the believer will be manifested with him in glory. Christ is our life; that is, he contains within himself the image and power of eternal life to be given through him to the believer; and the believer will be manifested with him in the same glory which he

---

[74] So Michaelis, *TWNT*, VI, 877.   [75] *TWNT*, VI, 878.
[76] The word and idea are repeated in verse 23.

now possesses. Finally, there are two passages which relate the act of Christ to the new humanity of the believer and which at the same time raise the troubling question of the meaning of the phrase ἐν Χριστῷ. 'Therefore, if any one is in Christ, he is a new creation' (II Cor. 5:17). 'For as in Adam all die, so also in Christ shall all be made alive' (I Cor. 15:22). These passages seem to point to the identity of eschatological existence between Christ and believer. While the motif does touch upon Paul's Adamic Christology, the problems involved are far too complex and would lead us too far afield to press further.[77]

The collective weight of these passages leaves no doubt that Paul equates the humanity of the exalted Christ with that of the man given the gift of eternal life. It is the Lord who makes possible this new existence, and in some way he mediates his own life to the believer. At this point, however, an important qualification must be made. Some, but not all, of these passages affirm that it is by Christ's own power that the believer receives his new existence. Paul can just as easily point to God as the source of the life to come. 'If the Spirit of him who raised Jesus from the dead dwells in you, he who raised Christ Jesus from the dead will give life to your mortal bodies also through his Spirit which dwells in you' (Rom. 8:11). In Rom. 8:30 it is God who predestines, calls, justifies, and glorifies. The apparent ambiguity here arises out of Paul's belief that God is the ultimate actor in everything that Christ performs.[78] Christ rules over all powers and will ultimately subdue death because God has subjected all things to him (I Cor. 15:24–28). The motif of Christ as agent of the new humanity thus stems, in the final analysis, out of

[77] Cf. the discussion in Robinson, *The Body*. W. D. Davies argues that the concepts of 'body of Christ' and 'in Christ' are influenced by rabbinic ideas about Adam. Since the rabbis teach that all mankind comes ultimately from the first man, 'Was it not natural, then, that Paul when he thought of the new humanity being incorporated "in Christ" should have conceived of it as the "body" of the Second Adam, where there was neither Jew nor Greek, male nor female, bond nor free' (*Paul and Rabbinic Judaism*, p. 57). The difficulty here is that the evidence he uses as support does not relate the unity of man in Adam with the *body* of Adam. The rabbis do acknowledge that all men sprang from Adam and that mankind is a unity, e.g., *M. Sanh.* 4.5. Almost all the sayings about Adam's *body*, however, relate the first man to the physical, not the historical world. The best evidence for Davies' view is both isolated and late; cf. *Exod. R.* XL. 3.

[78] E.g., II Cor. 5:19. Paul also usually speaks of God as the agent of Christ's resurrection, e.g. I Cor. 15:4, Rom. 6:4.

I

Paul's reflections about Christ's relationship with God. Since Paul can vacillate between God and Christ as agent, the idea that Christ out of his own power creates the new humanity is not absolutely necessary to the Adamic Christology. In fact it may not have belonged originally to the Adamic Christology at all.

Paul's main point may perhaps have been inspired by the Jewish motif of Adam as first patriarch of Israel.[79] Certainly Adam and Christ are the founders of two races of men, the mankind of death and the mankind of life. Each is the *Stammvater*, the original ancestor, of his particular humanity. For Paul, however, Adam is not the first patriarch of the chosen people. Just as he makes no use of the motif of Adam as portrait of true humanity, so he does not suggest any relationship between Adam and Israel. Israel is subsumed under the patriarchy of Adam only as a subdivision of the humanity of death.

For Paul the church is now the chosen people of God (Rom. 9:25) and may once even be labeled the 'Israel of God'.[80] Of this chosen people it is Christ who is the first-born of many brethren and the first-fruits.[81] Thus Paul may imply that Christ is the first patriarch of the new creation in his status as exalted, resurrected man. The antitheses in Rom. 5:15–21 suggest a contrast between the two heads. Adam mediates death to his brethren, while Christ, life. The one acted in disobedience; the other, in obedience. Stemming from these two acts are two radically different results affecting the offspring of the two founders. Eduard Schweizer has recently argued strongly that Christ is the *Stammvater* of the eschatological community.[82] Just as Adam determined the fate of his descendants, so Christ as the new *Stammvater* determines the fate of his followers.[83] Albert Schweitzer made essentially the same point some years ago when

---

[79] Cf. above, pp. 22f.,38-46.

[80] Gal. 6:16. This is not entirely certain. For a recent discussion cf. *IB*, X, 590f. Whether or not Paul uses the word Ἰσραήλ of the church, the idea is certainly present many places in his Epistles.

[81] I Cor. 15:20; Rom. 8:29; cf. also Col. 1:18.

[82] Eduard Schweizer, 'Die Kirche als Leib Christi in den Paulinischen Homologumena,' *ThL*, LXXXVI (1961), 169.

[83] Ibid. Schweizer, I believe, is incorrect when he asserts (col. 164) that Adam was a determiner of destinies, and that Paul simply takes over this idea from Judaism. I have already argued that this motif is almost entirely absent in rabbinic treatments of Adam and, further, that Paul believes each man decides his own fate.

he said that Christ is the Second Adam 'in consequence of His Resurrection, by which He becomes the Ancestor of those who are appointed to the resurrection.'[84]

At any rate, a reasonably close parallelism exists between Jewish logia about Adam as first patriarch and the statements about Christ by Paul. Just as Adam, for Judaism, exhibited in his original existence God's intent for Israel, so Christ is the reality of God's design for man and is the first patriarch of the new creation. Since Paul has clearly made such a transference with respect to the motif of true humanity, it is tempting to agree with Schweizer that Paul has done the same thing here. The motif of the first patriarch would, furthermore, explain more easily the close relationship Paul sees between the nature of Christ and that promised to the believer. Nothing can hide the fact, however, that all the evidence for such a transfer is at best implicit. The attractiveness of the suggestion rests upon its plausibility and upon the fact that it facilitates the understanding of the texts.

More central to Paul's theology is the connection between Christ as the life-giving Spirit and the spiritual body bequeathed the believer. The Spirit is the power (δύναμις, ἐνεργεία) of God which brings the new life to man and the world.[85] Paul usually affirms that Christ is the mediator of this power, indeed in a sense *is* this power, and thus brings to man his new existence. In I Cor. 15:45 he is the life-giving Spirit. According to II Cor. 3:18 the transformation of the believer into the image of God is accomplished by the 'Lord who is the Spirit'. In Phil. 3:21 the change is effected by the power (here ἐνεργεία) which Christ exercises. Since the Spirit is closely associated with power, it may be that this verse is affirming the role of the Spirit as does II Cor. 3:18.

The relationship of baptism to the gift of the new life is readily apparent. Yet whether and to what extent baptism is connected to Paul's Adamic Christology is a complex problem without a ready solution. Jervell has argued that the motif of Christ as εἰκών is embedded in baptismal conceptions.[86] Paul's understanding of baptism as a dying and rising with Christ is not, however, directly related to Christ as Last Adam. Certainly the

---

[84] *The Mysticism of Paul*, p. 167.
[85] Cf. I Cor. 2:4f., 12:4–6; *TWNT*, VI, 431f.
[86] *Imago Dei*, pp. 197–256.

proleptic resurrection of Christians in baptism unites them with
the True Man, but the key notion of the death has rather to do
with Paul's belief in the atoning death of Jesus, perhaps as the
righteous martyr.[87] Since for Paul it is Christ as πνεῦμα who
effects the gift of the new creation, one is tempted to see baptism
as the gift of the πνεῦμα, as does the author of Acts. In this case,
the rising with Jesus in baptism would be that event in which
began the new existence given by the life-giving Spirit. Linking
baptism with the Spirit makes Paul's thought very coherent. The
difficulty is that Paul himself does not seem to relate the two in any
significant way. Two passages in I Cor., 6:11 and 12:13, do join
baptism with the Spirit and may imply the gift of new life given
by the Spirit.[88] Yet they have the flavor of formulas or creeds,
which Paul does no more than to repeat. The crucial passage,
Rom. 6:1-11, not only does not mention the Spirit, but also it is
hard to find any word or phrase in it which could be taken as an
allusion to the Spirit.[89] Certainly baptism is that event in which
the believer, by participating in the resurrection of Christ, enters
the new creation. Paul, however, does not explicitly go any
further, and the simplest solution may be correct, that he does not
relate the motif of Last Adam with that of dying and rising with
Christ.

What is certain in the above is that (a) Christ as the reality of
God's intent for humanity and (b) the conformity of the believer
to this same humanity are centrally rooted in Paul's Adamic
Christology. Certain too is that Christ as the direct agent of this
humanity is also a part of the complex woven about the Last
Adam. That this idea originated in Paul's reflection about the
relation between Christ and Adam is not, however, as clear, and it
may be that here the complex interaction of the various motifs in
Paul's theology begins to be manifested. Whatever the source,
the result is a coherent unity not at all marred by the insistence of
Paul that behind the lordship of Christ lies the ultimate authority
of God.

[87] Cf. Scroggs, NTS, X (1963/64), 104–108.
[88] Cf. Héring, Corinthiens, pp. 45, 112.
[89] Rudolf Schnackenburg's attempt to make the relation through the phrase
'in newness of life,' ἐν καινότητι ʒωῆς, while not impossible, still strikes me as
somewhat desperate; see Das Heilsgeschehen bei der Taufe nach dem Apostel
Paulus (Munich, 1950), pp. 159–63.

TRUE HUMANITY AS PRESENT REALITY

The discussion above has primarily been concerned with the gift of life at the eschaton. Investigations in recent years, however, have assured us that Paul believed the day of the kingdom had dawned with the resurrection of Christ.[90] The kingdom of God is secretly, inwardly present within the believer now. The necessary corollary is that the restoration of man's humanity and the presence of the kingdom are inseparably connected. No sense can be made of realized eschatology in Paul that does not allow for the reality of man's eschatological existence as also a present phenomenon. The change in man must be as real as the presence of the kingdom itself.[91]

Paul in a few places does indeed suggest that the beginning of the new humanity has already taken place. The clearest example is found in II Cor. 3:18. 'And we all, with unveiled face, beholding the glory of the Lord, are being changed into his likeness from one degree of glory to another.' The present tense, μεταμορφούμεθα, indicates the transformation has already begun and is continuing, while the word itself has eschatological overtones elsewhere in the New Testament. It occurs, significantly, in the transfiguration narrative. Of this Behm writes: 'What the pious is promised for the new age happens to Jesus in the present.'[92] Since the new age

[90] E.g., Bultmann, *Theology*, I, 276; C. H. Dodd, *The Apostolic Preaching* (New York, 1951), p. 65.

[91] Much recent scholarship attempts to limit the present reality to a reality 'in faith' or 'of hope' or 'of obedience'. This view is perhaps most clearly seen in treatments of the Spirit in Paul, e.g, Schweizer, *TWNT*, VI, 422–31, and Käsemann, 'Der gottesdienstliche Schrei nach der Freiheit,' *Festschrift für Ernst Haenchen* (Berlin, 1964), pp. 142–55. As far as I can see, this exegesis is not based on an attempt to find a subjective reality for the new existence but rather on the understanding that man *is* what he *does*. I find this definition to be very attractive and persuasive as a modern way of looking at man, but I do not believe Paul thought in that way. The Apostle is thereby inaccurately modernized. There are here, it seems to me, two attendant exegetical dangers. 1. Despite the intent of this approach, the reality of the new existence *may* in practice by so subjectivized that the objective *extra nos* of the new being, its reality which exists apart from the frailty of human willing and loving, is lost sight of. 2. This means in turn that despite emphasis upon the new obedience, the high ethical expectation that Paul has for the Christian may in the final analysis not be taken seriously. Paul's thought moves in the realm of the substantial and objective as the ground for the new obedience, and without this ground there can be, for him, nothing either new or obedient about the life of the believer. H. Schlier rightly argues that the new life takes place both in faith and baptism. A knowledge comes out of the obedience of faith; but while this may illumine the believer about the new existence, it cannot create it. For this, baptism is necessary. Cf. Schlier, 'Vom Menschenbild des Neuen Testaments,' in *Der alte und der neue Mensch* (Munich, 1942), pp. 24–36.

[92] *TWNT*, IV, 765.

has already dawned for Paul, he knows that this transformation has actually begun.[93] Rom. 12:2f. contains essentially the same idea. 'Do not be conformed to this world but be transformed [μεταμορφοῦσθε] by the renewal of your mind, that you may prove what is the will of God, what is good and acceptable and perfect.' Here the relation to Adamic Christology is missing, but the use of μεταμορφόω and ἀνακαίνωσις (renewal) suggests an eschatological meaning. The νοῦς is not simply the intellectual faculty but the will of man as well; it is there that the Spirit has begun to restore man to his true nature. The verse further shows the close relation Paul sees between existence and ethics. The result of the transformation of the inner man is the restoration not only of nature but of man's authentic relation with God.

II Cor. 4:16 repeats the above idea in somewhat different words, although ἀνακαινόω is again present. 'Though our outer humanity [ἄνθρωπος] is wasting away, our inner humanity is being renewed every day' (translation mine). Col. 3:10 is similar. The new humanity *is* being renewed (again ἀνακαινόω) in knowledge according to the image of its creator. In all of these passages ἀνακαινόω implies that Paul is thinking of eschatological existence as a new creation. Christ as Last Adam is the first fruits of the new creation. Although the Christian still lives in 'this world' in his outer being, his inner life is made new by the Spirit, according to the nature of the resurrected Christ, who is the true image of God and thus the true reality of man. In light of the above, the reading of the subjunctive favored by the great majority of textual witnesses in I Cor. 15:49, φορέσωμεν, is made credible. 'Let us bear the image of the heavenly man.' Just as in Rom. 12:2 man is exhorted to 'be transformed', so here he is urged to accept the gift of the Spirit which is true humanity.[94]

---

[93] Cf. also Gal. 5:19.

[94] To the problem, whether the new existence takes place now in some specific part of man, no simple answer can be given. Bultmann's analysis of Paul's terms has shown well that words such as spirit (πνεῦμα), soul (ψυχή), mind (νοῦς), body (σῶμα), and flesh (σάρξ) in general denote the whole man seen from some specific aspect; cf. *Theology*, I, 192–239. This has often led exegetes to conclude that Paul never makes any distinctions within man like those made by Greeks and gnostics. It is clear that the Apostle had no regular *terminology* to signal such distinctions, for although there are passages where νοῦς and πνεῦμα seem to denote an inner, non-fleshly center of man's renewal, one can easily find other passages where the words are used more broadly (cf., e.g., Rom. 12:2 with I Cor. 14:13ff.). Yet Paul seems to be able to make a distinction, despite the lack of terminology, and one might well argue that

Finally, Paul describes the ethical life of transformed man as exhibiting the fruits of the Spirit (Gal. 5:16–25). Christ as Last Adam is the life-giving Spirit. While man in the new world will live a perfect existence, in this life he still exists in the ambigious situation of being a part of both worlds. Nevertheless, in so far as he is a new creature he is expected to bear fruits. Paul exhorts man to 'become what he is', to act out the life given him as a gift by the Last Adam. Existence and ethics are inseparably linked in Paul's thought, but neither can be dissolved into the other.

The picture of Paul's Adamic Christology is now complete. By a close comparison with his Jewish heritage the underlying functions to which the Apostle puts this Christology become clear. Through this language Paul describes the reality and assurance of the restoration of man's humanity. Lost by the sin of man himself, this humanity becomes a complete reality in the 'one man Jesus Christ', who is able to bestow it upon the believer because this one man is also the life-giving Spirit. While the complete realization of genuine life in a spiritual body awaits the final day, the believer has already been given the Spirit, has already died and been raised with Christ in baptism and, thus linked with the founder of the eschatological manhood, already partakes of the new nature. He is thus called upon to exhibit the fruits of this restored nature, living a life of obedience and love.

Since both the partial as well as the complete realization of this humanity depends upon God's gift of the resurrection, the restor-

---

this ability is especially significant just because he has no ready-made concepts. He points to the νοῦς as the center of renewal (Rom. 12:2), and the renewal in knowledge (εἰς ἐπίγνωσις) of Col. 3:10 probably means the same. He distinguishes between an outer and outer man in II Cor. 4:16, and in the midst of the very enigmatic passage, Rom. 7:13–25, equates νοῦς with the inner man (vss. 22f.). His distinction between flesh and blood and the spiritual body in I Cor. 15 also would seem to suggest that Paul differentiated between an outer, visible part of man and an inner, non-fleshly (but perhaps also material) part which is the eschatological man. Perhaps significant too is that in at least two of the passages where the presence of the eschatological nature is implied (II Cor. 3:18, Col. 3:10), the restoration of the image, which is certainly a non-corporeal concept for the Apostle, is mentioned. If the subjunctive of I Cor. 15:49 is correct, this would be a third. None of this is of course conclusive but I think it likely that Paul's sense of the presence of the new existence led him to begin to question where in man this reality was to be found, and this in turn forced him to make a rough and ready distinction between the inner and the outer, fleshly man, a distinction already at hand in Judaism, if not in the Old Testament. Obviously Paul did not reflect on the question enough to create a set terminology.

ation is not a human possibility as such. Even though Paul clearly thinks of eschatological existence as a 'nature', as a σῶμα, it is not any the less a free gift from God. Nor does this life become a permanent possession of man so that he might in some way control his own destiny. However much a demythologization of Paul may be necessary for the modern age, Paul for his own times guards well against both the hardening of the substantive gift—so that it becomes an indelible stamp of man apart from his response to God—as well as any attempt to evaporate the reality of the gift into a subjective experience (whether this be labeled emotional, volitional, or existential). The present reality of the humanity of Christ, although thought of in terms of a σῶμα, is nevertheless the total reality of man as God intended him to be and is a witness to the victorious achievement of this intent. 'But thanks be to God, who gives us the victory through our Lord Jesus Christ.'

ADDENDUM I

ADAM AS MICROCOSMUS

One motif about Adam's nature, not discussed in Chapter II because it is essentially unrelated to the argument, nevertheless needs to be mentioned. This is the notion of Adam as the *microcosmos*, implied in II Enoch 30:8–10, 13, and Sib. Oracles III. 24–26. II Enoch describes Adam's nature as coming both from corporeal and incorporeal substances. While the details of his statement may come from Stoic and Philonic ideas,[1] II Enoch differs from Greek thought in refusing to make a simple separation into soul and body which come from spiritual and physical sources respectively. Emphasized here is the Jewish view of the unified nature of man. The motif serves also partly as a kind of 'scientific' explanation of man's nature.[2] The parallel logia in II Enoch 30:13 and in the Sibylline Oracles describe how Adam's name was made from the Greek names of the four compass directions. W. D. Davies suggests that this motif indicates the 'universality or the unity of all mankind in him' (Adam).[3] The context of the logia, however, is not concerned with the historical order but the natural. Both of these sayings may thus be said to suggest that Adam is a microcosmos, although the term is not used. Just as Adam sums up in his nature the entire cosmos, so does his name.

Probably the main function of these motifs is to picture man as the acme of all of God's creative intent. All of creation has its

---

[1] Of the seven consistencies Charles says, 'This list of substances seems to have some connexion with Stoic speculation (G. Sext. Math. ix. 81) and Philonic views'; *Apoc. and Pseud.*, II, 448. For Philo he suggests that related passages are *Op. mundi* 40, 46, 51; *Leg. all.* ii.7. Charles also mentions Plutarch, *Plac.* iv.4. There are, however, rabbinic logia which relate Adam to both spiritual and physical substances. He is created with four attributes from above (stature, voice, vision, understanding) and four from below (eating, procreation, excretion, mortality); cf. *Gen. R.* VIII.11; XIV. 3. In this instance, however, the rabbinic parallels seem more remotely related than the Greek. It should be noted again that this passage is found in a MS tradition considered inferior by Vaillant. Cf. above, p. 23. n. 20.

[2] The author of II En. displays a keen scientific interest about natural phenomena throughout his writing. Rain, snow, dew, the order of the heavens, and the relation between sun and moon are some aspects of nature for which he gives explanations.

[3] *Paul and Rabbinic Judaism*, p. 55.

telos in man. One of the most difficult and yet exciting elements of Jewish theology is just this claim: despite the immense complexity of both visible and invisible creation, despite the apparent smallness and frailty of man, everything has been done on his account. It is crucial to note that here no proof exists that the concept of the *Urmensch* has infiltrated into the theology. The function of the *Urmensch* is diametrically opposed to the microcosmic motif. In some way the world comes to exist through the *Urmensch*. But here the opposite is the case. Man is not prior to the world; he is its climax. The world is not made from him; he is made from the world.[4]

[4] For a strong and accurate statement of the independence of Jewish thought about Adam from any essential *Urmensch* or Son of Man motifs, cf. Jervell, *Imago Dei*, pp. 39, 41.

ADDENDUM II

PHILO'S INTERPRETATION OF GENESIS 1–3

Hellenistic Judaism, in distinction from Jewish-influenced gnosticism and magic, developed no independent Adamic speculation. This is at least the judgment one must surely levy upon Wisdom of Solomon, II Enoch, and the works of Philo, those writings inevitably fallen back upon when the theology of Greek-speaking Jews is in question.[1] The few relevant sections of Wisdom of Solomon and II Enoch (cf. chap. II above) suggest nothing startlingly novel about Adam, and the discussion to follow should prove that when Philo writes about Adam as a concrete human figure he does nothing more than to rephrase Jewish tradition (interestingly enough, more rabbinic than apocalyptic) into Hellenistic concepts. Philo is, in fact, our earliest source for some of the rabbinic sayings. Perhaps the nearly total absence of Adamic motifs in the non-Pauline New Testament helps to confirm the lack of real interest in Adam among Hellenistic Jews.[2] There is, furthermore, no evidence that gnosticism has influenced the specific Adamic sections that are found in the Hellenistic Jewish materials. Peterson's attempt to see such a connection in Wisdom of Solomon 10:1f. is unconvincing,[3] and the points of contact which researchers find between Philo and *anthropos* speculations all have to do with the heavenly and earthly men, never with the first man.[4]

[1] Adam is almost never mentioned in other writings that are clearly Hellenistic and Jewish. Besides the reference in Sib. Oracles III.24–26 (cf. Addendum I), there is the uninspired treatment by Josephus in *Antiquities* I.32–52, 67–71. Josephus merely retells the biblical narrative of Adam and Eve, as seen through the eyes of early Judaism, spiced here and there by apocalyptic or rabbinic traditions. What this author really demonstrates is how little interested it was possible for a Hellenistic Jew to be in the Adamic materials.

[2] Outside of unimportant references to Adam in Luke 3:38, I Tim. 2:13f., and Jude 14, only Col. 1:15–20, Phil. 2:5–11, and Mark 1:9–11 could be considered Adamic in background, and not even these are certain.

[3] Cf. E. Peterson, 'La Libération d'Adam de l'Ἀναγκή,' *RB*, LV (1948), 211.

[4] E.g., C. H. Dodd, *The Fourth Gospel*, (Cambridge, 1958), pp. 69–71, and J. Pascher, *Der Königsweg zu Wiedergeburt und Vergöttung bei Philon von Alexandreia* (Paderborn, 1931), pp. 125–34.

Just on the issue of Philo's heavenly man, however, the
question has repeatedly been raised whether Paul is dependent on
Philo or Philonic-like ideas for his Adamic Christology, or whether
he is at least opposing such ideas in I Cor. 15:46: 'But it is not the
spiritual which is first but the physical, and then the spiritual'.
Paul's relationship with Hellenistic Judaism is a complex problem
and need not be treated here. He must have known some of the
literature of the diaspora Synagogue just as surely as he knew
rabbinic theology. The evidence is indeed overwhelming that
Paul was well acquainted with Wisdom of Solomon,[5] and the
possibility that Paul could have known the kind of thinking Philo
presents cannot be denied. As a matter of fact, however, the
significant differences between Paul and Philo—on eschatology
and anthropology, to name only two—would have made Paul's
appropriation of the Philonic system difficult indeed, and very few
actual similarities, not to mention direct clashes, between the two
writers are to be found. There is an even more specific reason why
the attempt to relate Paul and Philo on the heavenly man founders:
the usual exegesis of Philo on this subject misrepresents, in my
opinion, the thought of the Alexandrian. The grounds for this
contention must be investigated in some detail.

Philo's Exegesis of Genesis I

Scholars have been almost unanimously in agreement that
Philo uses the two accounts of creation in Gen. 1 and 2 to speak of
the creation of the heavenly man and the earthly Adam, respectively.[6] One lone dissenting judgment has come from B. Stegmann, who argues that both Gen. 1:26f. and 2:7 speak of the
creation of the actual first man, Adam, as united by a fusion of a
generic heavenly man and a generic earthly man.[7] While Stegmann's view is perhaps extreme and difficult to hold in its entirety,[8]
I believe it shows a direction more profitable to pursue than that
taken by the majority of scholars.[9] The results for our purpose are
important: the heavenly man is seen to be not a mythical personage

[5] Cf. J. Fichtner, *Weisheit Salomos* (Tübingen, 1938), p. 9.
[6] Cf. H. Wolfson, *Philo* (Cambridge, 1947), I, 310.
[7] *Christ, the 'Man from Heaven'* (Washington, 1927), pp. 19–48.
[8] Cf., e.g., J. M. Creed's review of *Christ, the 'Man from Heaven'* in *JTS*,
XXIX (1927/28), 310f. I do not, however, agree with all of Creed's criticism.
[9] This Addendum can only indicate the outline of my argument. For a
full discussion, see my dissertation, 'Adamic Christology,' pp. 253–76.

but one of the incorporeal ideas, and he is not contrasted with the first historical man.[10]

According to Philo God creates spontaneously and instantaneously. The world was not created in six days, and the account in Genesis is so arranged only because an orderly presentation is necessary. Gen. 1 is therefore not an historical narrative,[11] and Philo does not suggest that certain objects are temporally prior to others. He does say that the ideas are prior to their sensible counterparts, but this precedence seems by Philo's own admission to be logical or axiological rather than temporal, even though temporal terms are used to denote the distinction.[12] Day one describes the creation of all the incorporeal ideas.[13] This means that the 'heavenly man' as the idea of *nous* belongs to this day and not to the sixth.[14] Days two to six must be thus seen as describing the creation of the sensible world.[15] Gen. 1:26f. narrates neither the creation of a mythical man, nor the idea of *nous*, but the actual *nous* which forms the highest part of man's soul.[16] The context in *De opificio mundi* suggests this strongly. For example, Philo is in part concerned with the question: Why was man created last? The answers given imply that he is thinking here about the *nous* which belongs to individual man, not about *nous* as an incorporeal idea.[17]

[10]Although any individual statement by Philo might seem straightforward, it is obvious, once various passages are compared, that he can be inconsistent. At times there is even a bewildering confusion of terms and of uses to which these terms are put. For an analysis of those having to do with the heavenly and earthly men cf. E. Bréhier, *Les Idées philosophiques et religieuses de Philon d'Alexandrie* (2d ed.; Paris, 1925), pp. 121–24. To one who comes to Philo from haggadic literature, however, such lack of consistency is not surprising. Philo is not a speculative philosopher, although he *has* a speculative philosophy; nor is he a scientific biblical scholar. He is rather a religious thinker and his treatises should be read not as philosophy but as sermons or haggadah. Philo's inconsistencies arise where the religious point he is making forces a momentary slant of his philosophical terms or his exegesis. Thus to make a general, if tentative, statement about Philo's position is possible; to build an unassailable construction out of his writings is impossible.

[11] *Op. mundi* 13, 26–28, 67.

[12] Ibid., 16, 36, 69, 134.

[13] Stegmann, *Christ, the 'Man from Heaven,'* p. 21; *Op. mundi* 15f., 36f.

[14] For the heavenly man cf. *Leg. all.* i.31, 89.

[15] *Op. mundi* 36f.

[16] For the relationship between the idea of *nous* and the individual *nous* cf. *De plant.* 42; *De somniis* i.215; *Leg. all.* i.22.

[17] For example, man was created last so that he might come into his world with everything ready as a man comes to a banquet already prepared; cf. *Op. mundi* 77–86.

What, however, is the heavenly man and how is it related, on
the one hand, to the individual *nous* and, on the other, to the
Logos? Though Philo uses *nous* in various ways, these all stem
from the Alexandrian's basic conviction that the mind is the
'essential' man.[18] The idea of *nous* is indeed referred to as the
heavenly man.[19] He does not come into contact with matter.[20] He
never leaves the presence of God.[21] He is by nature incorruptible.[22]
He is neither male nor female.[23] Most importantly, the heavenly
man is made according to God's own nature, according to God's
image.[24] As such he is an ἰδέα, or γένος, or σφάγος, as well as
made κατὰ τὴν εἰκόνα.[25] Thus he is in direct lineage from God.

Now it is true that, in one sense, the heavenly man is no more
than one among many incorporeal ideas.[26] Yet in effect he is much
more. This 'man' is stamped with God's own image, and this
stamp is usually conceived to be the Logos. The boundary between
Logos and *nous* is extremely fluid and indicates the close relation to
essential deity which the latter seems to enjoy. It is true that God
does not share in rationality; he is rather its source.[27] The Logos,
however, is not only the image of God but the divine thought as
well.[28] Thus while the Logos contains within itself all the incorporeal ideas, that idea which comes closest to defining Logos is
that of *nous*. It is not too surprising to find passages where the
Logos and the heavenly man seem to be identified.[29] Thus the
heavenly man is a kind of mediator of God's essence—though
Philo is careful to guard himself against pantheism or the deification of man.[30] It is within this context that we are to understand
the phrase 'the true man', ὁ πρὸς ἀλήθειαν ἄνθρωπος. On the
one hand it denotes the divine *nous*;[31] but by participation of man's
individual *nous* in the heavenly *nous* each man contains within
himself the true man.[32] This is essential man, essential because
nous is God's image in man.[33]

[18] E.g., *Op. mundi* 69–71.
[19] The Platonic scheme of incorporeal ideas has been, of course, appropriated
by Philo.
[20] *Leg. all.* i.31.   [21] Ibid., 89.   [22] *Op. mundi* 134.
[23] Ibid.   [24] Ibid.   [25] Ibid.
[26] Cf. *Leg. all.* i.22 and *Op. mundi* 25.   [27] *Quod deterius* 82.
[28] *Op. mundi* 24–38.
[29] Cf. *De conf. ling.* 41,62f., 146f.; Dodd, pp. 70f.
[30]Although he is apparently tempted by such views, cf. *De plant.* 18f.;
De mutat. nom. 223; *De spec. leg.* iv.123.
[31] *De fuga* 71.   [32] *Quod deterius* 22; *De plant.* 42; *De somniis* i.215.
[33]Cf. *De mutat. nom.* 223.

So far then we have the following descending order: God, the source of *nous;* Logos, the divine thought, who both creates the incorporeal ideas and contains them all within himself; and the heavenly man, or ideas of *nous*, whose creation is described or implied on the 'first' day. The next level is the individual *nous*, or the highest part of man's soul, whose creation is described on the sixth day in Gen. 1:26f. This *nous* is not the earthly man, that is, not the man placed in opposition to the heavenly man. In *De opificio mundi* 69–71 Philo has inserted a lyric encomium about the human mind. Molded after a divine pattern, it is a god within man. Although Philo is tempted by the Stoic view that the *nous* is a particle of ether, he qualifies himself at the crucial moment.[34] It remains the true essential *man*, even though it is closely related to God through the heavenly man.[35] All these ideas seem to be philosophical rather than mythical in character and function.[36] While the idea of *nous*, and even occasionally the Logos, are labeled ἄνθρωπος, Philo does not appear to be thinking of a primordial man who functions in a cosmological or soteriological manner. If speculations about a mythical *anthropos* lie behind Philo's terminology, they have been essentially transformed and demythologized.

Philo's Exegesis of Genesis 2

The problem caused by the presence of what moderns call the second creation narrative is deftly handled by the Alexandrian theologian. Gen. 2:4–7 is a 'concluding summary' of Gen. 1.[37] This summary repeats the order found in Gen. 1 and thus proceeds from the incorporeal world to the creation of man. The man described in Gen. 2:7 is not, however, the same as that found in Gen. 1:26f. Led by an entirely different text with different concepts, Philo calls this man the 'earthly man'. 'There are two types [γένη] of men; the one a heavenly man, the other an earthly. The heavenly man, being made after the image of God, is altogether without part or lot in corruptible and terrestrial substance;

[34] Cf. note 30 above.
[35] *De plant.* 42; *De somniis* i.215.
[36] There are important ethical and epistemological aspects of the orders of *nous*, but it is impossible to treat them here. Cf. *Leg. all.* i. 38, 53–55, 88f., 105–108; ii. 49–56; iii. 44f.; *Quod deterius* 86; *Op. mundi* 154; *Quest. in Gen.* i.6.
[37] *Op. mundi* 129; so also Stegmann, *Christ, the 'Man from Heaven'*, p. 24, and Wolfson, *Philo*, I, 118f.

but the earthly one was compacted out of the matter scattered here and there.'[38] When Philo contrasts the heavenly man with some other object, Adam as the first historical man is not cited. What appears is rather the earthly man, the γήϊνος ἄνθρωπος. In *De opificio mundi* 134f. the earthly man denotes the composite mortal man with body and soul, who is either male or female. In the *Legum Allegoria*, on the other hand, the term refers to the earthly mind, a mortal substance connected with sense perception.[39] In either case the 'earthly man' represents an element which is joined to the higher *nous* described in Gen. 1:26. What must always be kept in mind is that for Philo Gen. 1f. presents a logical, not a temporal order. Thus the formation of the earthly man or the lower *nous* does not take place after the creation of the higher *nous*. It is simply described in a later section of Scripture.

Philo refuses, moreover, to take the story in Gen. 2:8–3:24 as an historical event. Speaking of the garden in Gen. 2, he writes: 'This description is, I think, intended symbolically rather than literally.'[40] The trees of the garden are symbols for virtues.

---

[38] *Leg. all.* i.31. The translations of Philo in this addendum are taken from the *Loeb Classical Library* edition, trans. F. H. Colson and G. H. Whitaker (London, 1929–41).

[39] The complications and perhaps inconsistencies involving the two different 'minds' are most likely caused by the two different exegetical complexes Philo uses. When dealing with Gen. 1:26f., he speaks of the image of God, and here the *nous* is immaterial and related to the heavenly man. When he uses Gen. 2:7 the immaterial part of man is the divine breath, while everything else, including *nous*, is mortal and corruptible. One may note here the difficult passage in *Leg. all.* i.32:

> We must account the man made out of the earth to be mind mingling with, but not yet blended with, body. But this earthlike mind is in reality also corruptible, were not God to breathe into it a power of real life; when He does so, it does not any more undergo moulding, but becomes a soul, not an inefficient and imperfectly formed soul, but one endowed with mind and actually alive.

Cf. also *Leg. all.* i.42, 88, 90–92. The implication, if one wishes to combine the two systems, is that there are two parts of the soul or mind: the lower, mortal part; and the part stamped with the divine image that is immortal. Cf. Stegman, *Christ, the 'Man from Heaven'*, p. 35. This view is supported by *De fuga* 69, where working from the Gen. 1:26f. system, he holds, inconsistently with other assertions, that these verses describe the creation of both the higher and the lower *nous*, here called soul:

> So the Father of all things is holding parley with His powers, whom He allowed to fashion the mortal portion of our soul by imitating the skill shown by Him when He was forming that in us which is rational, since He deemed it right that by the Sovereign should be wrought the Sovereign faculty in the soul, the subject part being wrought by subjects.

Cf. also *Quis rerum* 230–36 and *Op. mundi* 72–75.

[40] *Op. mundi* 154.

Adam represents the earthly mind. Eve is sensation. The serpent is pleasure. The serpent as pleasure lures sensation into its service and sensation then corrupts the mind. The mind turns away from virtue and, following after pleasure, becomes enslaved to it.[41]

The First Man

From what has been said, it should be clear that Philo in his exegesis of Gen. 1f. is not primarily interested in the 'historical Adam', and certainly not in contrasting him with a mythological Urmensch. Nevertheless Philo does believe that an actual first man once existed and uses rabbinic concepts to describe him. The first man was created with a uniquely superior body. He was of giant size and his senses were more perceptive than those of present mankind.[42] He was the one man truly 'beautiful and good' in body as well as soul.[43] In *De opificio mundi* 136–38, there are clear echoes of rabbinic logia about the size of Adam, his creation from the pure place of the earth, and the title, '*ḥallah* of the world'. Rabbinic is also the title 'first man' (=אדם הראשון). Philo reserves the proper name Adam for its symbolic meaning of earthly *nous*.[44]

The Alexandrian is more interested in describing the superior soul in Adam, who at his creation is the example of the truly virtuous man. 'Since the divine spirit had flowed into him in full current, he earnestly endeavoured in all his words and actions to please the Father and King, following Him step by step in the highways cut out by virtues.'[45] Adam was possessed with philosophical sight and hearing; that is, he was able to attain true religion and to know the incorporeal world.[46] 'For not inaptly do some conjecture that they [the first couple] were provided with eyes with which they could see those natures and beings and actions which were in heaven.'[47] Clearly the 'some' are the theologians who believed that Adam could see from one end of the earth to the other, and from the ground up to heaven.[48] In addition Philo enlists Adam as the only world citizen, μόνον κοσμοπολίτην,[49]

---

[41] Cf. *Op. mundi* 154; *Leg. all.* i.43 to end.
[42] *Quest. in Gen.* i.32; cf. also *Op. mundi* 136, 140, 145, 148; *De virt.* 203.
[43] *Op. mundi* 136.
[44] E.g., *Op. mundi* 136, 145.
[45] Ibid., 144.
[46] *Quest. in Gen.* i.32.
[47] Ibid.
[48] E.g., *jBer.* VIII. 12*b*; II En. 31:2.
[49] *Op. mundi* 142.

K

and follows the long-standing Jewish tradition of ascribing both wisdom and kingship to him.[50]

These examples should be sufficient to show that the material on Adam in Philo is separated from that about the heavenly man in at least three important ways. 1. Its origin. The Adamic logia are rabbinic, while the substance of the teaching about the heavenly man is Greek. 2. Its character. The Adamic materials are unabashedly mythical; those of the heavenly man are philosophic. 3. Its function. Here lies the crucial difference. The first man serves to show the perfect, ideal man, that can never more exist on this earth,[51] while the heavenly and earthly men are used to construct the ontology of every man.[52] Obviously all the complexities and inconsistencies in Philo's treatment of Gen. 1f., are not resolved by the above summary of his exegesis. Nevertheless it should be clear that this Scripture enables Philo to point to three separate aspects of his thought: anthropology (*nous*, heavenly man, earthly man), mythology (the first man), and the psychology of sin (the fall of the mind to sensation and pleasure). The Alexandrian makes no attempt to contrast the heavenly man with the first man, since the two motifs are used for different purposes and basically have nothing to do with each other. Nor is the heavenly man temporally prior either to the earthly man or to Adam, a fact which would be essential to the argument that Paul is opposing Philo in I Cor. 15:46. Thus the ideas found in Philo cannot be said to be the background or foil for Paul's argument.

---

[50] For wisdom cf. *Op. mundi* 148, 150; *Quest. in Gen.* i.20f; for kingship cf. *Op. mundi* 83, 88, 148; *Quest. in Gen.* i.20.

[51] Cf. *Op. mundi* 139.

[52] Another important function of the Adamic materials for Philo is that of describing the essence of sin as a turning from God towards falsehood, pleasure, and the self, but it has been impossible to discuss this here. Cf. *Quest. in Gen.* i.40–42; *Op. mundi* 165ff.; *Leg. all.* i, *passim; De cherubim* 64–66.

SELECTED BIBLIOGRAPHY

A. TEXTS AND TRANSLATIONS

Aboth de Rabbi Nathan. Edited by Solomon Schechter. Vienna, 1887.
The Apocrypha: Revised Standard Version. New York: Nelson, 1957.
Biblia Hebraica. Edited by Rudolf Kittel. Stuttgart: Württembergische Bibelanstalt, 1954.
BRAUDE, WILLIAM G. *The Midrash on Psalms.* 2 vols. New Haven: Yale University Press, 1959.
BURROWS, MILLAR. *The Dead Sea Scrolls.* New York: Viking, 1955.
CHARLES, R. H. (ed.). *Apocrypha and Pseudepigrapha of the Old Testament.* 2 vols. Oxford University Press, 1913.
The Dead Sea Scrolls of St. Mark's Monastery. Edited by Millar Burrows. Vol. 2. New Haven: The American Schools of Oriental Research, 1951.
EPSTEIN, ISIDORE (ed.). *The Babylonian Talmud.* London: Soncino, 1935–52.
ETHRIDGE, J. W. *The Targums of Onkelos and Jonathan ben Uzziel on the Pentateuch.* Vol. 1. London: Longmans, Green & Co., 1862.
FREEDMAN, H. and SIMON, M. (eds.). *Midrash Rabbah.* London: Soncino, 1939.
GINSBURGER, MOSES (ed.). *Das Fragmententhargum.* Berlin: Calvary, 1899.
The Holy Bible: Revised Standard Version. New York: Nelson, 1952.
Le Livre des secrets d'Hénoch. Paris: l'Institut d'études slaves, 1952.
MANSOOR, MENAHEM. *The Thanksgiving Hymns.* Leiden: Brill, 1961.
Mekilta. Edited by Jacob Lauterbach. 3 vols. Philadelphia: Jewish Publication Society, 1933–35.
Midrash Rabbah. Vilna, 1887.
Midrash Tanhuma. Jerusalem, 1953.
Midrash Tanhuma. Edited by Solomon Buber. Vilna, 1912.
Midrash Tehillim. Edited by Solomon Buber. Vilna, 1891.
Novum Testamentum Graece. Edited by Erwin Nestle. Stuttgart: Württembergische Bibelanstalt, 1956.
Pesikta de Rab Kahana. Edited by J. Mandelbaum. New York: Jewish Theological Seminary, 1962.
Pesikta Rabbati. Edited by M. Friedmann. Vienna, 1880.
PETERMANN, J. H. *Brevis Linguae Chaldaicae.* Berlin, 1872.
PHILO JUDAEUS. *Works.* Edited and translated by F. H. Colson and G. H. Whitaker. 9 vols. ('Loeb Classical Library.') London, 1929–41. 2 vols. of supplement translated by Ralph Marcus. London, 1953.
Pirke de Rabbi Eliezer. New York, 1946.
Septuaginta. Edited by Alfred Rahlfs. 2 vols. Stuttgart: Württembergische Bibelanstalt, 1952.
Sifra de be Rab. Edited by J. H. Weiss and J. Schlossberg. Vienna, 1862.
Sifre de be Rab. Edited by M. Friedmann. Vienna, 1864.
Talmud Babli. New York, 1957.
Talmud Jerushalmi. Berlin, 1920.
Targum Onkelos. Edited by Alexander Sperber. 'The Bible in Aramaic,' vol. 1. Leiden: Brill, 1959.
Testamenta XII Patriarchum. Edited by M. de Jonge. Leiden: Brill, 1964.

B. CRITICAL STUDIES

ALLO, E. B. *Première Épitre aux Corinthiens.* 2d ed.; Paris: Gabalda, 1956.
ALTHAUS, PAUL. *Der Brief an die Römer.* ('Das Neue Testament Deutsch.') 6th ed.; Göttingen: Vandenhoeck & Ruprecht, 1949.
ALTMANN, A. 'Gnostic Themes in Rabbinic Cosmology,' in *Essays in Honour of the Very Rev. Dr. J. H. Hertz.* Edited by I. Epstein, E. Levine & C. Roth. London: Edward Goldston, 1942.

124 BIBLIOGRAPHY

BARRETT, C. K. *A Commentary on the Epistle to the Romans.* ('Harper's New Testament Commentary.') New York: Harper, 1957.
—— *From First Adam to Last.* New York: Scribner's, 1962.
BARTH, KARL. *Christ and Adam.* Edinburgh: Oliver & Boyd, 1956.
BEGRICH, JOACHIM. 'Die Paradieserzählung: Eine literargeschichtliche Studie,' *ZAW,* IX (1932), 93–116.
BENTZEN, AAGE. *King and Messiah.* London: Lutterworth, 1955.
BLACK, MATTHEW. 'The Pauline Doctrine of the Second Adam,' *SJT,* VII (1954), 170–79.
BONNARD, P. *L'Épitre de Saint Paul aux Philippiens.* ('Commentaire du Nouveau Testament.') Neuchatel: Delachaux & Niestlé, 1950.
BORNKAMM, GÜNTHER. 'Paulinische Anakoluthe in Römerbrief,' in *Das Ende des Gesetzes.* 2d ed.; Munich: Kaiser, 1958.
BOUSSET, WILHELM. *Hauptprobleme der Gnosis.* Göttingen: Vandenhoeck & Ruprecht, 1907.
BRANDENBURGER, EGON. *Adam und Christus: Exegetisch-religionsgeschichtliche Untersuchung zu Römer 5, 12–21.* Neukirchen: Neukirchener Verlag, 1962.
BRÉHIER, ÉMILE. *Les Idées philosophiques et religieuses de Philon d'Alexandrie.* 2d ed.; Paris: J. Vrin, 1925.
BRUNNER, EMIL. *The Letter to the Romans.* Translated by H. A. Kennedy. London: Lutterworth, 1959.
BUDDE, KARL. *Die biblische Paradiesesgeschichte.* Giessen: Töpelmann, 1932.
—— *Die biblische Urgeschichte.* Giessen: Ricker, 1883.
BULTMANN, RUDOLF. 'Adam and Christ according to Romans 5,' in *Current Issues in New Testament Interpretation.* Edited by W. Klassen and G. F. Snyder. New York: Harper, 1962.
—— 'ΔIΚΑΙΟΣΥΝΗ ΘΕΟΥ,' *JBL,* LXXXIII (1964), 12–16.
—— *Primitive Christianity in its Contemporary Setting.* Translated by Reginald H. Fuller. New York: World Publishing Company, 1962.
—— *Theology of the New Testament.* Vol. 1. Translated by Kendrick Grobel. New York: Scribner's, 1954.
—— 'Ursprung und Sinn der Typologie als hermeneutischer Methode,' in *Pro Regno Pro Sanctuario.* Edited by W. J. Kooiman and J. M. Van Veen. Nijkerk: Callenbach, 1950.
BURNEY, C. F. 'Christ as the ARXH of Creation,' *JTS,* XXVII (1926), 160–77.
CERFAUX, LUCIEN. *Le Christ dans la théologie de Saint Paul.* Paris: Editions du Cerf, 1951.
COLPE, CARSTEN. *Die religionsgeschichtliche Schule.* Göttingen: Vandenhoeck & Ruprecht, 1961.
CREED, J. M. Review of Basil Stegmann, *Christ, the 'Man from Heaven,'* in *JTS,* XXIX (1927/28), 310–11.
—— 'The Heavenly Man,' *JTS,* XXVI (1924–25), 113–26.
CULLMANN, OSCAR. *The Christology of the New Testament.* Translated by S. G. Guthrie and C. A. M. Hall. Philadelphia: Westminster, 1959.
DAHL, N. A. 'Christ, Creation and the Church,' in *The Background of the New Testament and its Eschatology.* Edited by W. D. Davies and D. Daube. Cambridge University Press, 1956.
DAVIES, W. D. 'The Jewish Background of the Teaching of Jesus: Apocalyptic and Pharisaism,' *ET,* LIX (1947–48), 233–37.
—— *Paul and Rabbinic Judaism.* 2d ed.; London: S.P.C.K., 1955.
—— 'Paul and the Dead Sea Scrolls: Flesh and Spirit,' in *The Scrolls and the New Testament.* Edited by Krister Stendahl. New York: Harper, 1957.
DIBELIUS, MARTIN. *An die Thessalonicher I. II. An die Philipper.* ('Handbuch zum Neuen Testament,' Vol. 11.) 3d ed.; Tübingen: J. C. B. Mohr, 1937.
DITTMANN, WILHELM. 'Die Auslegung der Urgeschichte (Gen. 1–3) im Neuen Testament.' Microfilm. Dissertation, Göttingen, 1953.
DODD, C. H. *The Apostolic Preaching.* New York: Harper, 1951.
—— *The Epistle to the Romans.* ('Moffatt New Testament Commmentaries.') New York: Harper, n. d.
—— *The Fourth Gospel.* Cambridge University Press, 1958.

DRIVER, S. R. *The Book of Genesis.* ('Westminster Commentaries.') London: Methuen & Co., 1904.

DRUMMOND, JAMES. *Philo Judaeus.* 2 vols. London: Williams & Norgate, 1888.

DUBARLE, A. M. *Le Péché originel dans l'Écriture.* Paris: Les Editions du Cerf, 1958.

DUPONT-SOMMER, A. 'Le Testament de Lévi (xvii–xviii) et la secte juive de l'Alliance,' *Semitica,* IV (1952), 33–53.

ELTESTER, F. W. *Eikon im Neuen Testament.* Berlin: Töpelmann, 1958.

ENGNELL, IVAN. ' "Knowledge" and "Life" in the Creation Story,' in *Wisdom in Israel and in the Ancient Near East.* Edited by Martin Noth. ('Supplements to Vetus Testamentum,' Vol. 3.) Leiden: Brill, 1955.

—— *Studies in Divine Kingship in the Ancient Near East.* Uppsala: Almqvist & Wiksells, 1943.

FICHTNER, J. *Weisheit Salomos.* Tübingen: J. C. B. Mohr, 1938.

FOERSTER, WERNER. 'Der heilige Geist in Spätjudentum,' *NTS,* VIII (1961–62), 117–34.

FRANKFORT, HENRI, et al. *The Intellectual Adventure of Ancient Man.* Chicago: University of Chicago Press, 1946. Published in Great Britain as *Before Philosophy.* Harmondsworth, Middlesex: Penguin, 1951.

FUCHS, ERNST. *Christus und der Geist bei Paulus.* Leipzig: Hinrichs, 1932.

GEORGI, DIETER. 'Der vorpaulinische Hymnus Phil. 2, 6–11,' in *Zeit und Geschichte.* Edited by Erich Dinkler. Tübingen: J. C. B. Mohr, 1964.

GRESSMANN, HUGO. 'Die Paradiessage,' *Festgabe von Fachgenossen und Freunden A. von Harnack.* Tübingen: J. C. B. Mohr, 1921.

GUIGNEBERT, Ch. 'Quelques remarques d'exégèse sur Philippiens, 2, 6–11,' *RHPR,* III (1923), 512–23.

GUNKEL, HERMANN. *Genesis.* ('Handkommentar zum Alten Testament.') 3d ed.; Göttingen: Vandenhoeck & Ruprecht, 1910. Reprinted, Vandenhoeck & Ruprecht, 1964.

—— *Schöpfung und Chaos in Urzeit und Endzeit.* Göttingen: Vandenhoeck & Ruprecht, 1895.

HAENCHEN, ERNST. 'Gab es eine vorchristliche Gnosis?' *ZTK,* XLIX (1952), 316–49.

HÉRING, JEAN. 'Les Bases bibliques de l'humanisme chrétien,' *RHPR,* XXV (1945), 17–40.

—— 'Kyrios Anthropos,' *RHPR,* XVI (1936), 196–209.

—— *La Première Épître de Saint Paul aux Corinthiens.* ('Commentaire du Nouveau Testament.') Paris: Delachaux & Niestlé, 1949.

HOOKE, S. H. (ed.). *Myth, Ritual, and Kingship.* Oxford: Clarendon Press, 1958.

HOOKER, M. D. 'Adam in Romans I,' *NTS,* VI (1959–60), 297–306.

HUMBERT, PAUL. *Études sur le récit du paradis et de la chute dans la Genèse.* Neuchatel: Secretariat de l'Université, 1940.

The Interpreter's Bible. George Buttrick, General Editor. 12 vols. New York: Abingdon, 1952–57.

JACOB, EDMUND. *Theology of the Old Testament.* Translated by A. W. Heathcote and P. J. Allcock. New York: Harper, 1958.

JASTROW, MORRIS. 'Adam and Eve in Babylonian Literature,' *American Journal of Semitic Language and Literature,* XV (1899), 193–214.

JERVELL, JACOB. *Imago Dei: Gen. 1, 26f. im Spätjudentum, in der Gnosis und im den paulinischen Briefen.* Göttingen: Vandenhoeck & Ruprecht, 1960.

JONGE, M. DE. 'Christian Influence in the Testaments of the Twelve Patriarchs', *Novum Testamentum,* IV (1960), 182–235.

JÜNGEL, E. 'Das Gesetz zwischen Adam und Christus,' *ZTK,* LX (1963), 42–74.

KÄSEMANN, ERNST. 'Der gottesdienstliche Schrei nach der Freiheit,' in *Festschrift für Ernst Haenchen.* Berlin: Töpelmann, 1964.

—— 'Gottesgerechtigkeit bei Paulus,' *ZTK,* LVIII (1961), 367–78.

—— 'Kritische Analyse von Phil. 2, 5–11,' in *Exegetische Versuche und Besinnungen.* Vol. 1. Göttingen: Vandenhoeck & Ruprecht, 1964.

126 BIBLIOGRAPHY

KÄSEMANN, ERNST. *Leib und Leib Christi.* Tübingen: J. C. B. Mohr, 1933.
—— 'Zur Thema der urchristlichen Apokalyptik,' *ZTK*, LIX (1962), 257–84.
KITTEL, GERHARD (ed.). *Theologisches Wörterbuch zum Neuen Testament.*
  Stuttgart: Kohlhammer, 1933 and continuing.
KITTEL, HELMUTH. *Die Herrlichkeit Gottes.* Giessen: Töpelmann, 1934.
KRAELING, CARL. *Anthropos and Son of Man.* New York: Columbia University
  Press, 1927.
KÜHL, ERNST. *Der Brief des Paulus an die Römer.* Leipzig: Quelle und Meyer,
  1913.
KÜMMEL, W. G *Das Neue Testament: Geschichte der Erforschung seiner Probleme.*
  Freiburg: Karl Alber, 1958.
KUSS, OTTO. *Der Römerbrief.* 2d ed.; Regensburg: Pustet, 1963.
LARSSON, E. *Christus als Vorbild.* Lund: Gleerup, 1962.
LIETZMANN, HANS. *An die Korinther I. II.* ('Handbuch zum Neuen Testa-
  ment', Vol. 9.) 4th ed.; Tübingen: J. C. B. Mohr, 1949.
—— *An die Römer.* ('Handbuch zum Neuen Testament' Vol. 8). 4th ed.;
  Tübingen: J. C. B. Mohr, 1933.
LIGHTFOOT, J. B. *St. Paul's Epistle to the Colossians.* London: Macmillan,
  1876.
LIGIER, LOUIS. *Péché d'Adam et péché du monde.* Paris: Aubier, 1960.
LODS, ADOLPHE. Review of Paul Humbert, *Études sur le récit du paradis et de la
  chute dans la Genèse,* in *RHPR*, XXV (1945), 71–78.
LOHMEYER, ERNST. *Kyrios Jesus. Eine Untersuchung zu Phil. 2, 5–11.* ('Sitzungs-
  berichte der Heidelberger Akademie der Wissenschaften,' Phil.-hist.
  Klasse, No. 18.) Heidelberg, 1928.
MCKENZIE, J. L. 'The Literary Characteristics of Gen. 2–3', *Theological
  Studies,* XV (1954), 541–72.
MARMORSTEIN, A. 'Paulus und die Rabbinen,' *ZNW*, XXX (1931), 271–85.
MASSON, CHARLES. *L'Épître de Saint Paul aux Colossiens.* ('Commentaire du
  Nouveau Testament.') Neuchatel: Delachaux & Niestlé, 1950.
MAY, HERBERT. 'Some Cosmic Connotations of Mayiim Rabbim, "Many
  Waters",' *JBL*, LXXIV (1955), 9–21.
MEYER, R. *Hellenistisches in der rabbinischen Anthropologie.* Stuttgart: Kohl-
  hammer, 1937.
MICHAELIS, WILHELM. *Zur Engelchristologie im Urchristentum.* Basel: Majer,
  1942.
MICHEL, OTTO. *Der Brief an die Römer.* ('Kritisch-exegetischer Kommentar.')
  Göttingen: Vandenhoeck & Ruprecht, 1963.
MOFFATT, JAMES. *The First Epistle of Paul to the Corinthians.* ('Moffatt New
  Testament Commentaries.') New York: Harper, n.d.
MOORE, GEORGE F. *Judaism.* 3 vols. Cambridge: Harvard University Press,
  1927.
MOULE, C. F. D. *The Epistles of Paul the Apostle to the Colossians and to
  Philemon.* ('Cambridge Greek Testament,' N.S.) Cambridge University
  Press, 1957.
MOWINCKEL, SIGMUND. *He That Cometh.* Translated by G. W. Anderson.
  Oxford: Blackwell, 1956.
—— *The Two Sources of the Predeuteronomic Primeval History (JE) In Gen.
  I–II.* ('Avhandlinger utgitt av det Norske Videnskaps-Akademi i Oslo,'
  II Hist.-Fil. Klasse.) Oslo, 1937.
MÜLLER, CHRISTIAN. *Gottes Gerechtigkeit und Gottes Volk.* Göttingen: Vanden-
  hoeck & Ruprecht, 1964.
MURMELSTEIN, BENJAMIN. 'Adam, ein Beitrag zur Messiaslehre', *Wiener
  Zeitschrift für die Kunde des Morgenlandes,* XXXV (1928), 242–75, and
  XXXVI (1929), 51–86.
NEUGEBAUER, F. *In Christus.* Göttingen: Vandenhoeck & Ruprecht, 1961.
NÖTSCHER, F. 'Geist und Geister in den Texten von Qumran', in *Mélanges
  bibliques en l'honneur de André Robert.* Paris: Bloud et Gay, 1957.
—— *Zur theologischen Terminologie der Qumran-Texte.* Bonn: Hanstein, 1956.

NYGREN, ANDERS. *Commentary on Romans.* Translated by Carl Rasmussen. Philadelphia: Muhlenberg Press, 1949.
PASCHER, J. *Der Königsweg zu Wiedergeburt und Vergöttung bei Philon von Alexandreia.* Paderborn: Schöningh, 1931.
PEDERSEN, JOHANNES. *Israel I–II.* London: Milford, 1926.
PETERSON, E. 'La Libération d'Adam de l'Ἀναγκή,' *Revue Biblique,* LV (1948), 199–214.
PFEIFFER, R. H. *History of New Testament Times.* New York: Harper, 1949.
QUISPEL, G. 'Der gnostische Anthropos und die jüdische Tradition,' *Eranos Jahrbuch,* XXII (1953), 195–234.
RAD, GERHARD VON. *Genesis.* Translated by John H. Marks. Philadelphia: Westminster, 1961.
—— *Old Testament Theology.* Vol. I. Translated by D. M. G. Stalker. New York: Harper, 1962.
RAWLINSON, A. E. J. *The New Testament Doctrine of the Christ.* London: Longmans, Green & Co., 1926.
REITZENSTEIN, RICHARD. *Die hellenistischen Mysterienreligionen.* 3d ed.; Stuttgart: Teubner, 1956.
Die Religion in Geschichte und Gegenwart. Edited by Kurt Galling. 3d ed.; Tübingen: J. C. B. Mohr, 1957–62.
RENGSTORF, K. H. *Die Auferstehung Jesu.* Witten-Ruhr: Luther Verlag, 1954.
ROBERTSON, ARCHIBALD AND PLUMMER, ALFRED. *First Epistle of St. Paul to the Corinthians.* ('International Critical Commentary.') New York: Scribner's, 1911.
ROBINSON, J. A. T. *The Body: A Study in Pauline Theology.* ('Studies in Biblical Theology', No. 5.) Naperville: Allenson, 1951.
RÖSSLER, DIETRICH. *Gesetz und Geschichte.* 2d ed.; Neukirchen: Neukirchener Verlag, 1962.
RUSSELL, D. S. *The Method and Message of Jewish Apocalyptic.* Philadelphia: Westminster, 1964.
SANDAY, WILLIAM AND HEADLAM, ARTHUR. *The Epistle to the Romans.* ('International Critical Commentary.') 5th ed.; Edinburgh, 1902.
SCHECHTER, SOLOMON. *Some Aspects of Rabbinic Theology.* New York: Macmillan, 1923.
SCHLIER, HEINRICH. *Galaterbrief.* ('Kritisch-exegetischer Kommentar.') 12th ed.; Göttingen: Vandenhoeck & Ruprecht, 1962.
—— 'Vom Menschenbild des Neuen Testaments,' in *Der alte und der neue Mensch.* Munich, 1942.
SCHMIDT, HANS. *Die Erzählung von Paradies und Sündenfall.* Tübingen: J. C. B. Mohr, 1931.
SCHMIDT, HELMUT. *Die Anthropologie Philons von Alexandreia.* Würzburg: Triltsch, 1933.
SCHMITHALS, WALTER. *Die Gnosis in Korinth.* Göttingen: Vandenhoeck & Ruprecht, 1956.
SCHNACKENBURG, R. *Das Heilsgeschehen bei der Taufe nach dem Apostel Paulus.* Munich: Zink, 1950.
SCHWEITZER, ALBERT. *The Mysticism of Paul the Apostle.* Translated by William Montgomery. New York: Macmillan, 1955.
SCHWEIZER, EDUARD. 'Die Kirche als Leib Christi in den paulinischen Homologumena,' *ThL,* LXXXVI (1961), cols. 161–74.
SCOTT, E. F. *The Epistles of Paul to the Colossians, to Philemon, and to the Ephesians.* ('Moffatt New Testament Commentaries.') New York: Harper, 1930.
SCROGGS, ROBIN. 'The Adamic Christology of Paul in the Light of his Jewish Heritage.' Microfilm. Dissertation, Princeton University, 1962.
—— 'The Exaltation of the Spirit by Some Early Christians,' *JBL,* LXXXIV (1965), 370–73.
—— 'Romans VI. 7,' *NTS,* X (1963–64), 104–8.
SKINNER, JOHN. *Genesis.* ('International Critical Commentary.') New York: Scribner's, 1910.

STAERK, W. *Die Erlösererwartung in den Östlichen Religionen. Soter II.* Stuttgart: Kohlhammer, 1938.
—— *Soter I. Der biblische Christus.* Gutersloh: Bertelsmann, 1933.
STEGMANN, BASIL. *Christ, the 'Man from Heaven'.* ('Catholic University of America New Testament Studies', No. 6.) Washington, 1927.
STEIN, EDMUND. *Philo und der Midrasch.* Giessen: Töpelmann, 1931.
STRACHAN, R. H. *The Second Epistle of Paul to the Corinthians.* ('Moffatt New Testament Commentaries.') New York: Harper, n.d.
STRACK, HERMANN AND BILLERBECK, PAUL. *Kommentar zum Neuen Testament aus Talmud und Midrasch.* 6 vols. 2d. ed.; Munich: Beck, 1954–61.
TENNANT, F. R. *The Sources of the Doctrines of the Fall and Original Sin.* Cambridge: Cambridge University Press, 1903.
THACKERAY, HENRY ST. JOHN. *The Relation of St. Paul to Contemporary Jewish Thought.* London: Macmillan, 1900.
VERMÈS, GÉZA. *Discovery in the Judean Desert.* New York: Desclee, 1956.
VINCENT, M. R. *Epistles to the Philippians and to Philemon.* ('International Critical Commentary.') New York: Scribner's, 1897.
VOLZ, PAUL. *Die Eschatologie der jüdischen Gemeinde.* Tübingen: J. C. B. Mohr, 1934.
WEISS, JOHANNES. *Der erste Korintherbrief.* ('Kritisch-exegetischer Kommentar.') 9th ed.; Göttingen: Vandenhoeck & Ruprecht, 1910.
WERNBERG-MØLLER, P. *The Manual of Discipline.* Leiden: Brill, 1957.
WIDENGREN, GEO. 'Early Hebrew Myths and their Interpretation', in *Myth, Ritual and Kingship.* Edited by S. H. Hooke. Oxford: Clarendon, 1958.
WILCKENS, U. 'Die Bekehrung des Paulus als religionsgeschichtliches Problem,' *ZTK,* LVI (1959), 273–93.
—— *Weisheit und Torheit.* Tübingen: J. C. B. Mohr, 1959.
WILLIAMS, N. P. *The Ideas of the Fall and of Original Sin.* London: Longmans, Green & Co., 1917.
WINDISCH, HANS. *Der zweite Korintherbrief.* ('Kritisch-exegetischer Kommentar.') 9th ed.; Göttingen: Vandenhoeck & Ruprecht, 1925.
WOLFSON, HARRY A. *Philo.* 2 vols. Cambridge: Harvard University Press, 1947.

INDEXES

I. Bible

A. OLD TESTAMENT

B. NEW TESTAMENT

II. Apocrypha, Pseudepigrapha, Qumran, and Philo

A. APOCRYPHA AND PSEUDEPIGRAPHA

B. DEAD SEA SCROLLS

C. PHILO

III. Rabbinic Literature

MISHNAH

TALMUD BABLI

TALMUD JERUSHALMI

MIDRASH RABBAH

MEKILTA

SIFRA

SIFRE TO DEUTERONOMY

Midrash Tehillim

Pesikte de Rabkahana

Pesikta Rabbati

Midrash Tanhuma

Midrash Tanhuma, Ed. Buber

Pirke de Rabbi Eliezer

Aboth de Rabbi Nathan

Targumim

Koheleth Zuta

IV. Subject and Author

138　　　INDEXES

227.06
Scr4
c.l.

Date